NEW PERSPECTIVES IN SPECIAL EDUCATION

It is now widely believed in many western countries that the segregation of students with special educational needs is problematic, and that wherever possible these students should be educated alongside their peers in regular education settings. There has been a general move towards integrating special and regular education into one system that caters for a much wider range of students. But the outcomes in various countries have been very different. This book describes and evaluates these outcomes in the hope that teachers and other professionals may be able to profit from each other's experiences.

The book provides both quantitative and qualitative information, analysing the similarities and differences between integration practices in six western countries: Italy, Denmark, Sweden, the United States, England and Wales, and the Netherlands. The concluding chapters summarise the findings and offer some general conclusions. The authors discuss the factors that are critical to integration from a teacher perspective, and explore the aims and limitations of integration.

Cor J. W. Meijer is Deputy Director of the Institute for Educational Research, RION, University of Groningen, the Netherlands. He is a member of the OECD/CERI group of experts for the project *Integration in the School*. **Sip Jan Pijl** is a senior researcher, also at RION. He is involved in research on teacher planning, instruction and evaluation practices of teachers, the diagnosis of learning problems of students, and innovations in special education. **Seamus Hegarty** is Deputy Director of the National Foundation for Educational Research in England and Wales. He is also a member of the OECD/CERI group of experts for the project *Integration in the School*. He acts as a consultant to UNESCO and is Editor of the *European Journal of Special Needs Education*.

NEW PERSPECTIVES IN SPECIAL EDUCATION

A six-country study of integration

Edited by Cor J. W. Meijer, Sip Jan Pijl and Seamus Hegarty

Dutch–English translations and editorial assistance by Inge Abbring

London and New York

First published 1994
by Routledge
11 New Fetter Lane, London EC4P 4EE

Simultaneously published in the USA and Canada
by Routledge
29 West 35th Street, New York, NY 10001

© 1994 Cor J. W. Meijer, Sip Jan Pijl and Seamus Hegarty

Typeset in Palatino by Michael Mepham, Frome, Somerset
Printed and bound in Great Britain
by Biddles Ltd, Guildford and King's Lynn

British Library Cataloguing in Publication Data
A catalogue record for this book is available from the
British Library.

Library of Congress Cataloging-in-Publication Data
New perspectives in special education: a six-country
study/edited by Cor J.W. Meijer, Sip Jan Pijl, and Seamus
Hegarty.
p. cm.
Includes bibliographical references and index.

1. Special education–Europe–Cross cultural studies. 2.
Special education–United States–Cross-cultural studies. 3.
Handicapped–Education–Europe–Cross-cultural studies. 4.
Handicapped–Education–UniteD States–Cross-cultural
studies. 5. Mainstreaming in education–Europe–
Cross-cultural studies. 6. Mainstreaming in
education–United States–Cross-cultural studies. I. Meijer,
Cor J.W. II. Pijl, S.J. III. Hegarty, Seamus.
LC3986.A2N49   1994
371.9'04–dc20   93–10754
                                                                   CIP

ISBN 0–415–08336–2

CONTENTS

NOTES ON CONTRIBUTORS

Inge Abbring was attached as an educational researcher to the Special Education Section of the Institute for Educational Research, RION, University of Groningen, the Netherlands, from 1984 till 1989. She participated in several studies on the education of special needs children, including the study *Comparative Analysis on Special Education* (the CASE-project). She is now a freelance translator/editor in English and is also working in the book-trade.

Seamus Hegarty (PhD) is Deputy Director of the National Foundation for Educational Research in England and Wales. He has conducted extensive studies of provision for pupils with special needs in ordinary schools and has published widely on the topic. He is a member of the OECD/CERI group of experts for the project *Integration in the School* and acts as a consultant to UNESCO. He edits the *European Journal of Special Needs Education*.

Cor Meijer (PhD) is Deputy Director of the Institute for Educational Research, RION, University of Groningen, the Netherlands. He has conducted several studies on special education and integration (including the CASE-project). He is a member of the OECD/CERI group of experts for the project *Integration in the School*. He is also a member of the Groningen Centre for Comparative Education.

Sip Jan Pijl (PhD) is a senior researcher at the Institute for Educational Research, RION, University of Groningen, the Netherlands. He is specialised in research in special education. He is involved in research on teacher planning, instruction and evaluation practices of teachers, the diagnosis of learning problems of students and innovations in special education. He is a member of the Groningen Centre for Comparative Education.

Jan Rispens (PhD) is a professor of special education at the University of Utrecht, the Netherlands. His research area is dyslexia and developmental disorders. In 1987 and 1988 he participated in the CASE-project at the Institute for Educational Research, RION, University of Groningen.

ACKNOWLEDGEMENTS

Several individuals and institutions helped us to realise this book. We would like to express our gratitude to: the Institute for Educational Research in the Netherlands, SVO, for their grant for the study that forms the basis of this book; UNESCO for their grant for the translation and editing of the original Dutch reports; the co-writers of earlier versions of the country descriptions: Inge Abbring, Alie Houwing and Bouwe Span (Institute for Educational Research, RION); the reviewers who kindly looked at drafts of the country descriptions: Kenneth Eklindh, Nora Ferro, Jørgen Hansen and Kenneth Kavale; all the respondents we have interviewed in Italy, Denmark, Sweden, the United States, England and Wales and the Netherlands; all the schools that opened their doors to us and gave us the opportunity to learn from their integration experiences.

We also wish to thank Conny Lenderink for her administrative and editorial support for this book in the RION Institute.

Finally, we wish to express our gratitude to Inge Abbring for her help in different phases of the writing of this book. She participated in the RION research group that conducted the Dutch research which forms the basis of the book, and as editorial assistant she translated drafts into English.

Cor J. W. Meijer
Sip Jan Pijl
Seamus Hegarty

INTRODUCTION

Sip Jan Pijl and Cor J. W. Meijer

GOAL OF THIS BOOK

In most countries in the western world special schools have been founded for the education of students with special needs. For many decades educators and administrators in these countries have put a great deal of effort into developing a thorough and widely accepted system of special schools. Students, parents, the educational community and society as a whole were proud of their facilities for students with special needs. In a way the system expressed their care for these groups of students.

Gradually however, this view of special education has changed. The knowledge, expertise and school facilities are still things to be proud of and to preserve, but the segregation of students with special needs is widely perceived to be problematic. Many people believe that these students should be educated alongside their peers in regular education settings to the greatest extent possible. This means that special and regular education have to be integrated into one system that caters for a wide range of students and their (special) needs.

The integration of students with special needs into regular education and – in a wider context – the integration into society of all kinds of segregated groups have been debated in the last decades throughout practically the whole western world. Yet, the outcomes have been very different. Today we are faced with a large diversity of organisational models, expertise and experiences in the attempts to reduce segregation in education. It is worthwhile describing this diversity and evaluating the outcomes in order to extend our knowledge base on integration in education and in order to be able to profit from each other's experiences. That is the goal of this book on integration.

To write a book on the state of the art of integration in education is necessary and at the same time naïve. Integration is a process, not an outcome. As stated explicitly in the Scandinavian countries, but not only there, one must always try not to segregate individuals or groups of individuals. This effort is a process that never ends. There are always individuals or groups of individuals that are threatened by marginalisation and one should be constantly aware of this possibility. The naïvety then is clear: an accurate account of the state of the art of a process like integration is a chimera. Integration is an ongoing process and describing it as a steady state violates reality.

This exactly reflects the feeling we had in writing this book. In writing on integration issues the notion of historiography is explicit and inevitable. It is like a snapshot of an arrow in flight. Once studied it is already history. Of course this holds true for many phenomena in the social sciences but we had the impression that in studying integration it was especially pertinent. The countries we visited were all actively concerned with integration and change was occurring very rapidly.

Nevertheless we hope that our snapshots of integration practices and processes in different countries generate some insights that will assist colleagues in reflecting on their practice of integration and help to secure improvements in it.

CONTENT OF THE BOOK

This book focuses on the state of the art of integration in six western countries: Italy, Denmark, Sweden, United States, England and Wales, and the Netherlands.

Integration has become one of the central issues in (special) education. Within the context of the UNESCO, the EC (for example the 'Helios-project'), and the OECD (for example the 'Active life for disabled youth: Integration in the school' project), the integration of children with special needs into regular schools is a major policy concern. The number of books, conferences and integration projects is already large and still growing.

Efforts to realise more integrated settings have resulted in very different educational arrangements in different countries. These arrangements have been the focus of much attention in debates on integration and in turn necessitate changes in organisational structures, the curriculum, teacher training, and the legislative framework. There has been considerable exchange of information about developments in these topics. However, very little is known about the success of integration in regular education settings. This lack of knowledge is remarkable because the integration of students with special needs within regular education is strongly promoted and generally accepted as a desirable goal. This book is an attempt to fill that gap in knowledge. It provides both qualitative and quantitative information and analyses the similarities and differences between integration practices in different countries.

In Chapter 1, *Framework, Methods and Procedures*, Meijer and Pijl elaborate the conceptual framework of the study. The concept of integration is defined in terms of social and curricular integration. The chapter deals with the methodology that is used and sets it within the context of comparative research. It also addresses the selection of countries and the data gathering procedures.

In Chapter 2, *Italy*, Abbring and Meijer describe the situation of integration in Italy.

In Chapters 3, 4 and 5, Pijl discusses integration in respectively *Denmark, Sweden*, and the *United States*.

Hegarty addresses integration in *England and Wales* in Chapter 6.

The final country description is by Meijer who discusses the current integration situation in the *Netherlands*.

In Chapter 8, *Analysis of Findings*, Pijl and Meijer summarise the findings from both a quantitative and a qualitative perspective. They first give a short summary of the country descriptions and then group the six countries into three subgroups according to their policy. The last section of this chapter deals with the general conclusions that can be drawn from the findings in the six countries.

In Chapter 9, Hegarty discusses the factors that are critical to integration from a teacher perspective. He elaborates on the importance of teacher variables in providing appropriate, high quality education for pupils with special needs in regular schools.

Rispens, finally, discusses in Chapter 10 the aims and limits of integration. He deals with the goals that are to be achieved and the motives behind integration and argues that the vagueness and multiplicity of integration concepts and goals make it difficult to get a clear measure of the effects of integration practices.

1

FRAMEWORK, METHODS AND PROCEDURES

Cor J. W. Meijer and Sip Jan Pijl

COMPARATIVE EDUCATION RESEARCH

Writing about the state of the art of integration in a number of countries implies writing about differences. It is obvious that countries differ in the goals and means concerning the integration of students with special needs. Countries differ in their educational systems, in the educational goals set for students, in the history of education, in student populations, in teacher training, and so on. More than this, countries also differ in very many aspects outside education, for instance in population composition and density, gross national product per capita, legislation and moral values.

Quite a number of these differences affect education in one way or another and thus affect integration. For example, high population density facilitates the establishment of separate special schools (enough students at hand to fill them) and a high gross national product per capita enables a government to spend large(er) amounts of money in education. These relationships make it difficult to interpret the differences and similarities in education between countries. Two countries with a similar educational organisation (for instance, relatively high levels of individual tutoring in regular education) may have entirely different rationales for that particular type of organisation, e. g. large budget for education versus strong teacher attitudes towards integration.

Comparing countries in order to come up with general knowledge about education and to formulate do's and don'ts is therefore difficult. Yet, the wealth of information potentially available on the experiences of different countries is not to be neglected and, despite all the difficulties involved, it is worthwhile to describe and use it.

1

Questions about education in an international or cross-cultural context are typically the subject of comparative education. Niessen and Peschar (1982) distinguish three reasons why comparative research is undertaken. First, it is to answer the question: what is the situation like elsewhere and what do we know about it? Second, the aim of collecting information about countries may be directed towards problem solving or policy making within one's own country. Here it is hoped that after examining foreign educational systems and practices, features that are worth introducing in one's own system (or, conversely, that should be avoided at all costs) may be discovered. The third purpose follows theoretical interests. The goal is to investigate through comparative studies relationships between the various aspects of education. The question here is: what theoretically relevant relationships can be specified (Niessen and Peschar, 1982; Øyen, 1990).

Policy makers and practitioners all over the world are eager to learn from the experiences with integrated settings in other countries. But, learning from experiences in other countries means learning about relationships between variables. You do not learn much if you know that in Denmark 5 per cent of the students follow an intensive course, or, that in Sweden the education of two-thirds of the mentally handicapped takes place within the regular school. You learn something if you know that all the students who follow an intensive course in, for instance, reading, afterwards are able to follow the regular curriculum with their peers, or that the mentally handicapped in Swedish regular schools are socially integrated. The question is not what the pure facts are and what kind of instructional arrangements are made for the handicapped, but what effects the different arrangements have. Only then can a knowledge base be developed and decisions taken about the usefulness of these arrangements in changing one's own system (Antal, Dierkes and Weiler, 1987). So, a description of factors important in integration must lead on to an account of the relationships between these factors and their implications for integration.

As mentioned before, the countries described in this book differ in many respects. It is often argued that comparative analyses suffer from methodological difficulties. Comparability (or lack of it) is important in constructing research instruments and in drawing on elements of other educational systems to use in one's own system. Research instruments – for instance questionnaires – need to be as robust as possible in the face of differences between systems. For example, concepts like 'the learning disabled' and 'the support teacher' can have very different meanings in different countries.

When borrowing aspects of practice that have been successful in one context, for instance the Swedish working unit or the English outreach class, it is important not to overlook the country-specific factors that may have contributed to its success. Unless these differences between countries are taken into account, comparative studies have little value.

Comparative studies require equivalence: equivalence focuses on the relationships between a general dimension – for instance: a concept like social integration – and different indicators for it – for instance: placement in regular education and teacher attitudes (Niessen and Peschar, 1982). Equivalence implies that the same set of indicators relates to the general dimension. Equivalence is absent if a concept in different countries relates to different sets of indicators. In fact, we then have two different theories to explain our concept, and comparative research really becomes difficult then. In this view, comparability requires a theoretical underpinning in which the relationships between the variables of interest to the researcher are related to each other. A comparative analysis only makes sense if this theory can be applied in each of the countries involved.

In summary, comparative educational research aimed at extending our knowledge base on integration has to be based on an appropriate theory of integration. This theory should be applicable to each of the countries involved (equivalence). In gathering the data comparability of the information is essential.

The aim of this book, as presented in the Introduction, is to describe and evaluate the experience of integration in different countries. This implies a description of, among other things, referral and placement procedures, the organisation of regular and special education, instructional arrangements for children with special needs within regular education, and support and facilities for teachers in integrated classrooms. Our guiding theory is that the level of integration of students with special needs ultimately depends on the teacher and on the attitudes of parents and students.

Teacher behaviour is dependent on the resources available to

3

the teacher. These resources can be deduced from the micro-economics of teaching (Brown and Saks, 1987; Gerber and Semmel, 1985). In micro-economic theories three groups of resources are described: time, skills and materials. These resources exist as a result of, among other things, legislation policy, the organisation of special education, teacher training, regulations and conditions, number of students and the available curricula. Together with teacher attitude these can explain how teachers organise the education of a student with special needs and the integration level of students with special needs in education.

The attitudes of parents and students – most likely a reflection of prevailing attitudes in society – are further important factors in the integration of students with special needs. It is probable that in most western countries teacher resources and the attitudes of the people involved determine to a large extent the integration level of students with special needs.

The comparative analyses in this book operate within this general theory. Not all of the elements mentioned above are included in the analyses. The country descriptions concentrate on subjects like policy and legislation in (special) education, the organisation of (special) education, the provision made and teacher attitudes. In the country descriptions these subjects and the (level of) integration are described, and especially in the last chapters a number of comparative analyses are made.

DESCRIPTIVE FRAMEWORK

The term 'integration' is generally used as a collective noun for all attempts to avoid the segregated and isolated education of students with special needs. In the description of these attempts integration is conceived in terms of the organisational structure and in terms of the nature of integration.

In a review of studies on integration Hegarty, Pocklington and Lucas (1981) summarise the organisational possibilities as follows:

a   regular class, no support;
b   regular class, in-class support for teacher and student;
c   regular class, pull-out support;
d^1 regular class as basis, part-time special class;
d^2 special class as basis, part-time regular class;

4

e   special class full-time;
f   special school part-time, regular school part-time;
g   special school full-time.

Variants 'b' to 'f' are the possible forms in which integration can be organised. The extra support (as in variant 'b' or 'c') can be very different: for a physically handicapped student this may be the presence of an aide, for a visually or hearing impaired student the visit of an itinerant teacher, for an emotionally disturbed student extra support for the teacher (for further details see for instance Mittler, 1988).

The Hegarty *et al.* classification is in fact a mixture of at least three different organisational dimensions. It presents a continuum in terms of the distance to regular education, of the amount of extra instruction in the presence of non-handicapped students and of the amount of special support. This type of classification (see also Bruun and Koefoed, 1982; Emanuelsson, 1985; Söder, 1984) does not necessarily give information about the extent of student integration. A student in a regular classroom with a lot of extra support (variant 'c') might well be less integrated than a student from a special class who participates in part of the instruction in the regular classroom (variant 'f').

To describe the organisational variation in terms of actual student integration we use a classification based on the work of Kobi (1983). Kobi developed a model in which the phases of integration and the level of integration are combined. The phases of integration concern the degree to which integration has been realised. The first phase refers to the situation in which the intention to integrate students with special needs has been expressed. The second phase arises when a number of local projects experimenting with integration have been established. In the third phase the integration of students with special needs in regular education settings has become normal practice.

The level of integration is divided into six stages:

1   Physical integration. The architectural arrangements facilitate contact between handicapped and non-handicapped.
2   Terminological integration. Labelling and discriminatory expressions for the handicapped are not used.
3   Administrative integration. Handicapped students are encompassed within the same legislative framework as other students

(there can of course be large differences between the regulations on, for instance, support arrangements, transport and achievement levels).

4   Social integration. Social contacts between handicapped and non-handicapped students are frequent and intensive.
5   Curricular integration. The same curriculum framework and long-term goals apply for handicapped and non-handicapped students.
6   Psychological integration. All students are instructed together: that is, in one room, at the same time and using the same programme.

It is clear that integration involves considerable changes within and outside schools. It implies for instance a different attitude towards students with special needs in society, the revision of statutory regulations and funding systems, modifications to school buildings, transport facilities, organisation of common leisure activities, teacher training and curriculum development.

These activities are interdependent to some degree: one is not likely to create transport facilities or modify school buildings without some form of funding, or to develop new teacher training programmes or teaching programmes for students with special needs in regular education if statutory regulations hinder the admission of these students to regular education, and statutory regulations will not change unless attitudes in society change. This interdependence between the several factors is basically what Kobi (1983) expresses in his model. Kobi specifies a number of levels in a process, levels that build upon each other: entering a new level does not imply that the components of earlier levels can be discarded.

We used Kobi's line of thinking to specify three levels in the process of integrating students with special needs in regular education: segregation, social integration and curricular integration. Segregation entails quite separate education systems: not only special schools but also self-contained classes linked with regular education which in practice do not allow satisfactory social contact between students with special needs and their peers in regular education. With social integration we refer to every integrated situation in which the students receive major parts of their education outside the regular classroom but are still able to have substantial contact with their peers. With curricular integration we refer to educational settings in which children with special needs and their peers work together in curricular activities at the same time, at the same place and with the same teacher. However, part-time segregation for one or more curricular activities is not excluded.

In this model social integration precedes curricular integration. The rationale is simple: it is much easier to create opportunities for social contact between children with special needs and their peers within schools than to teach them together in the same classroom and with the same teacher. Social integration itself, though valuable, is not the ultimate goal of an integration process. The ultimate goal of integration within schools is that all students are members of one – not segregated – group of students in a classroom setting. Curricular integration in our concept and in our analysis should then include social integration. If this is not the case, we do not label it as curricular integration.

METHODOLOGY

In this book an attempt is made to describe the state of the art of integration in six different countries. The selection of countries is based on several criteria. In the first place there should be a clear policy towards integration. Though the practice of integration may differ, as well as the degree to which integration is accomplished, there should be a clear integration policy. A second criterion refers to the availability of information. This means that a number of countries are not included in our study because of the difficulty of obtaining information on integration. The third criterion can be described as the need to obtain a *variety* of integration models and practices. We were looking for countries that differ in their policy and practice. Nevertheless the countries should not differ too much with respect to socio-economic and cultural dimensions. These considerations have led to the selection of the following countries: Italy, Denmark, Sweden, the United States, England and Wales and the Netherlands.

The data presented in this book are based on the comparative study of the current practice of integration by a research team of the Institute for Educational Research (RION) of the University of Groningen (Abbring, Meijer and Rispens, 1989a, 1989b). In this study several country reports were made of which six countries have been selected for the purposes of this book. The country reports were based on an extensive study of literature (articles, policy papers, statistical data, etc.). They give a description of the structure of the educational system, the place of special education in it, policy and legislation, organisation and the state of the art of integration. In the second phase of the study key persons were interviewed. In each country key persons in research, policy making, teacher education and coordinating functions at the local level were approached. Also teachers, head teachers and professors of education were interviewed. In this second phase the information in the country reports was verified and additional data on the current practice of integration were gathered. Much attention was paid in the expert interviews to the state of the art of integration. In particular the following information was gathered:

1 The state of the art of integration: different models of integration, pupil categories, numbers of pupils, research and statistics with respect to integration.
2 The general practice of integration: experiences and problems with referral and placement, school and classroom management, teacher training, funding and so on.
3 Local integration projects: in the expert interviews we paid attention to examples of good practice in the different countries. Local integration projects were visited and key persons who were involved in these local projects were interviewed.
4 Integration policy: legislation, regulations, long-term and short-term policy, future developments.

In the third phase the country descriptions – if necessary changed through the second phase procedure – were verified and disseminated in several ways. In the first place the data were presented at several international congresses. Through discussions with experts and key persons in the different countries, the country reports were verified again and changed if necessary. In the second place the country reports were sent to several key persons in the countries concerned in order to get feedback on the quality of the descriptions. The descriptions presented in this book are the result of this process.

2

ITALY

Inge Abbring and Cor J. W. Meijer

INTRODUCTION

In the seventies the number of schools for special education decreased rapidly in Italy, as far as public education was concerned. The majority of students with special needs now attend regular education. There are now only a small number of schools left for physically, sensorily and mentally handicapped pupils. The most important measure that has been taken to make it possible to educate children with special needs in the regular school was the introduction of the so-called support teacher.

THE EDUCATIONAL SYSTEM

Structure

Public pre-school education for children from 3 to 5 years old (non-compulsory and free) has been legally established only since 1968. Before that time it was provided by churches and private institutions (Eurydice, 1986; Wielemans, 1987). In the middle of the eighties about 50 per cent of this age group attended non-state schools, sometimes on a fee-paying basis.

Despite its non-compulsory character, virtually all 5-year-olds nowadays attend pre-school education, though there are substantial differences between the northern and southern parts of Italy in this respect (Eurydice, 1986). In the year 1985/6, 87.8 per cent of pupils between 3 and 5 years of age attended a nursery school. Most nursery schools consist of three classes, corresponding to the three age groups, but classes with different age groups are allowed. A

9

class may contain thirteen to thirty pupils. If there is a handicapped pupil in the class, it may contain ten to twenty pupils (Bürli, 1985). The Montessori approach still has influence, but is often mixed with new insights (Wielemans, 1987).

Elementary education is compulsory (and free) for children from 6 to 14 years and comprises two cycles: primary education for children from 6 to 11 years and lower secondary education (comprehensive school) for children from 11 to 14 years (Bürli, 1985; Eurydice, 1986; OECD, 1985). These two educational levels are separated, not only spatially but also in terms of teacher education and curricula. As a result, there is little continuity in the elementary school system (OECD, 1985). However, since 1988 the governments made some efforts to link the two levels (Circular of January, 1988). For example, it has become possible for primary support teachers to follow handicapped pupils in lower secondary classes, in order to cope with transition problems (Ferro, 1992).

The most important characteristics of compulsory elementary education are:

1   A national curriculum; pupils have to be taught in three main subject areas and are examined at the age of 11. Teaching methods and the way in which examinations take place are determined locally.
2   The composition of classes is based upon mixed ability, in the primary as well as in the comprehensive school.
3   Instruction is teacher-centred; education takes place in small groups sometimes, but peer group tutoring, project work and individual programmes are exceptional.
4   The school-leaving examination of the comprehensive school can be adapted to the educational programme of the school (Bowman, Wedell and Wedell, 1985).

Nowadays, the basic organisational model in primary schools consists of three teachers for two classes. Each teacher is responsible for one main subject area. Forms of co-teaching, remedial teaching and other arrangements are used within this model, according to the needs of the class (Ferro, 1992).

The three-year comprehensive school has a common curriculum spread over 30 hours per week. Optional subjects and subsidised educational activities may add 10 or more hours per week in some well-organised schools. There are six teachers per class, one for each main subject. Pupils are taught in eight subjects and are examined at the age of 14. The comprehensive school certificate gives entrance to each school and institution of secondary education of the second grade (Wielemans, 1987).

Higher and university education are offered by private (fourteen) as well as public (thirty-five) institutions. High schools of different kinds take five years and are mostly public. The duration of university studies varies from four to six years, leading to a doctorate. So-called diploma courses are shorter and usually take two or three years.

Legislation, administration and policy

The Italian Republic functions at four levels: state, region, province and municipality. There are nineteen regions and eighty-four provinces. The state departments involved in education are the Department of Education, the Department of Public Health and the Department of Social Affairs (Bürli, 1985).

The Secretary of State for Education is assisted by a number of ministers. At the ministerial level there are nine directorates that are each responsible for a certain field of education (such as primary education). Another important division at the ministerial level is the 'Ufficio Studi e Programmazione' that coordinates research initiatives, in-service training of teachers and educational experiments (Eurydice, 1986). A special bureau is concerned with pre-school education.

The Secretary of State is not only head of the central educational administration, but also chair of the National Council for Public Education, the principal advisory body for all educational matters below the tertiary level (there is a separate university council for the tertiary level). This council is elected and consists of seventy-one members, appointed for five years, of whom 75 per cent are teachers. The council decides on school activities and services and draws up educational programmes. The Secretary of State has to submit all bills and important governmental questions to the Council (Eurydice, 1986).

Apart from the public education system there is a whole system of independent schools, administered by cities and municipalities, and private schools. All these schools also have to comply with national laws and decrees.

The organisation of pre-school education is to a large extent still in the hands of Roman Catholic congregations, but in primary and secondary education only 7 per cent of the pupils attend Catholic schools.

From 1970 the regional authorities were given a new status and were offered greater autonomy. The central power of the state was decentralised and delegated to regional authorities in a number of policy areas, such as health care (Ferro, 1992). Education as such remained centralised. Legislation, curricula and general administrative regulations are centrally determined. At the provincial level the Department of Education operates through the 'Provveditorati agli Studi' (ibid.). These local offices have authority over state schools (but not over universities). The 'Provveditorati' have administrative functions such as the allocation of class and support teachers, the planning of education, inspections and so on. They also coordinate, plan and support integration (ibid.). The inspectors are advised by the provincial school councils (eighty-four) that consist of fifty members who represent teachers, parents, unions, provincial and local authorities (Eurydice, 1986). These councils have existed since 1974 and are elected every three years. Their main task is to make recommendations on the way the educational needs of the community in question can be met. They serve as a bridge between school and community and are involved in the organisation of school guidance, medical and psychological services, and adult education (Bowman, Wedell and Wedell, 1985).

At the local level the primary schools are often grouped under an 'education circle'. Each circle may include two or more schools. The grouping into circles is made on a provincial basis. A school circle is led by a director (or head teacher) who is appointed by the state and has to stimulate and coordinate the activities of the various institutes that are involved.

The nursery school has its own administration, but falls under the responsibility of the head teacher of the primary school, in co-operation with educational inspectors who are assigned to the district for this purpose (OECD, 1985).

Compared to other EC countries Italy has had the most government shifts since the Second World War. There have been numerous reform plans, covering education as much as other areas. There is a progressive policy, but it is not always implemented (OECD, 1985). This can be explained by, among other things, regional differences in development, particularly between the prosperous and industrialised north and the most southern part of the country that is relatively poor (Wielemans, 1987).

As has already been mentioned, pre-school education has only been provided for by law in 1968. The law in question (444/1968) formed an important start for the reform of the education of children from 3 to 5 years. A large disadvantage, however, was the lack of regulations regarding the implementation of this law; this caused confusion and waste of energy with regard to both educational offering and educational planning.

The first important law with regard to primary education was the Coppino Act (1877) on compulsory four-year primary education (Wielemans, 1987). From 1922 till the end of the Second World War, Italy was ruled by a fascist regime that left its own mark on the educational reforms in that period. Between 1923 and 1928 (the Gentile reform), educational provision with regard to the classification of schools, educational inspectors, legal status of primary school teachers and so on, was laid down in royal decrees.

The new constitution of 1948 heralded a new era. It proclaimed the democratic right to at least eight years' free education for everyone (6 to 14 years) without any distinction of status, sex, political or religious conviction (Wielemans, 1987).

From 1971 profound changes took place in the legislation with implications for the integration of pupils with special needs into regular education (which will be further discussed in the next sections).

The realisation of the Italian comprehensive school in 1962 (Act 1859/1962) can be considered the most important policy decision in the post-war educational evolution, a decision that was part of a long-range plan which included other educational reforms (Wielemans, 1987).

The introduction of the uniform, compulsory and free comprehensive school would have to put an end to the existence of the elite schools, social discrimination and premature school choice. It would not be until 1977, however, that this new school concept was actually realised (Bürli, 1985).

During the past twenty years discussions on educational reform in Italy have been focused mainly on the upper part of the comprehensive school. In 1963 a parliamentary committee of inquiry drew up a reform programme for higher secondary education and the universities, for the period 1965–75. In 1968, however, the legislation in question was concluded without any concrete results (Wielemans, 1987).

SPECIAL NEEDS EDUCATION

Historical developments

Compared to other European countries, special education was introduced relatively late in Italy. For a long time the care and upbringing of children with special needs had not been considered a task of the school; in the towns the task was left to churches and charity, while in the country these children were mainly taken care of by their family. They often worked as farm-hands or herdsmen. Many children in the country did not go to school because their assistance on the land was urgently needed. Moreover, small municipalities were not obliged to found schools (Bianchi, 1984).

The education of children with special needs in Italy did not start until 1923, when special education was introduced by Act 3126/1923. Compulsory education was extended to blind and deaf-mute children. For the latter the compulsory school age was up to 16 years. These regulations were confirmed again in the elementary education act of 1928. Mentally handicapped children and children with severe behavioural problems were excluded from school attendance (Lunetta, 1987). Not only were schools for special education founded, mainly for blind and deaf pupils (the latter, by the way, had to move over to regular education after the fourth grade), but also classes for special education, in which learning disabled and behaviourally disturbed children were taken care of (Bianchi, 1984). These 'classes', however, bore more the character of detention centres than of schools (Lunetta, 1987). The religious institutions for blind and deaf-mutes were turned into schools that were recognised by the state.

The situation hardly changed during the fascist regime, when legislation came about that would continue till the end of the sixties. Only from 1933 on (Act 786/1933), when elementary education was delegated from the municipalities to the state, were schools for special education established at the state level. Act 786/1933 was the last act on special education till the Second World

War. Bianchi (1984) distinguishes three periods in the development of special education following the war:

1945–68

Until 1958 virtually no change took place. From 1958 there was an enormous expansion of special education. In 1960/61 the number of pupils in special classes was 0.35 per cent of the total number of pupils in elementary public education. In the following years their number grew and in 1967/68 they made up 1.23 per cent of the total population of elementary school children. Between 1961 and 1970 the number of pupils in special schools rose from 24,151 to 66,404; the number of special classes increased from 967 to 6,626 and the number of pupils in special classes grew from 13,768 to 60,670 (Galliani, 1982).

The causes of this growth must be sought in the economic development after the Second World War: not only did the employment structure change, but also increasing urbanisation took place, which resulted in an enormous population drift from south to north. These phenomena increased the marginalisation of weaker individuals.

Furthermore, educational organisation was founded upon the belief that education can best take place in homogeneous groups. This led to separate classes for special education for each type and each degree of handicap; in short, the system of special education became more and more differentiated (Jørgensen, 1980; Lunetta, 1987).

By presidential decree 1518/1967 guidelines were given for the school medical service and it was laid down that mildly mentally handicapped, socially unadjusted and behaviourally disturbed children, for whom replacement in regular education might be considered, could be placed in so-called 'differential' classes (Lunetta, 1987). Besides, it was laid down in Act 444/1968 on pre-school education, that nursery schools would be provided with special departments for learning disabled, behaviourally disturbed, mentally handicapped and sensorily handicapped children and that there would be special nursery schools for the more severely handicapped children (Lunetta, 1987).

1969–74

The growth of special education would undoubtedly have proceeded if the public opinion on education had not changed. This opinion was especially strong in organisations of parents of handicapped pupils, who were convinced that the education of handicapped pupils should not be based on the formation of homogeneous groups but on differentiation of education and treatment. This change of opinion must be seen in the context of a more general cultural movement that had its roots in the sixties. The most important components of the resulting reform were:

— health care reform (prevention, rehabilitation, anti-psychiatry);
— reorganisation of social services ;
— closer co-operation between schools and social services;
— closer co-operation between schools and labour market;
— decentralisation of state service (Bürli, 1985).

In the early seventies public opinion began to influence politics. The fight against the schools and classes for special education had started and the first experiences with integration were made.

1975–now

This was the time of reform. Classes and schools for special education were closed on the basis of the integration principle; a massive integration of pupils with special needs into regular education took place.

Legislation on integration

The development of the integration legislation concerning elementary education can be characterised as complex, manifold and contradictory (Bürli, 1985). The literature on this subject yields a substantial number of laws, decrees, circulars and so on, which does not make it easy to decide which are the most relevant ones. Nevertheless, we will try to give an overview of the most essential legislation on integration.

In 1971 the Italian parliament passed an act on social welfare which had implications for integration (Act 118/1971). From the heated discussions on education in those days the view emerged that integration of handicapped pupils is only possible if they are already prepared for it in the first years of life (handicapped children are given priority in the admission to crèches) and in the important socialisation phase of the primary school. Act 118 prescribes that the education of handicapped children must take place in regular classes of regular schools. Pre-school and primary education, but also lower and higher secondary education, should become more accessible to handicapped children. The law stated that compulsory education should take place in regular classes of public schools except for those children who suffer from severe mental or physical impairments that make regular education impossible or very difficult. However, the law did not define the degree of severity in an objective way, which in fact left placement decisions to the parents, the school and professional staff (Ferro, 1992).

According to Act 118/1971 all the necessary measures have to be taken to enable handicapped pupils to attend the regular school, such as free transport and removing obstacles in and around the school building (Guidi, 1986). For four to five years the Act did not really have a direct effect, but it did give the impetus to a broad discussion. Moreover, numerous provinces started to take up handicapped children in regular education between 1971 and 1974. These experiments mainly took place in the north and centre of Italy. Emilia-Romagna was the only region that implemented integration in a coordinated way in several cities (Bianchi, 1984).

A ministerial circular (227/1975) prescribed the integration of handicapped pupils for a group of schools in each province (nursery school, primary school and comprehensive school). In the legislation of 1975 (laws, circulars) further measures were formulated to stimulate the influx of handicapped pupils into regular schools: a thorough registration of all handicapped pupils, a maximum of twenty pupils in integration classes, a maximum of two handicapped pupils per class, support by the social–psychological–pedagogical service, flexible daytime education in regular classes and the formation of working groups at the education offices, whose task is to study problems in the field of integration and to make contact with teams of experts, parent organisations, remedial teachers and head teachers (Bürli, 1985; Lunetta, 1987; OECD, 1985).

According to Circular 227/1975 it was no longer possible to

exclude a child from regular education on the basis of the severity of a handicap, whereas this was still possible under Act 118/1971 (Hegarty, Pocklington and Lucas, 1981). While chronological age had always been the criterion for the admittance of handicapped children to pre-school education, Circular 235/1975 made it possible to take the mental age into account as well, so that children above the age of 6 could also enter the nursery school.

With a view to the danger of 'wild integration' a committee was set up in 1974 under the chairmanship of senator Falcucci, which had to lay the foundations of Act 517/1977, an education reform act in which the integration of handicapped pupils would be laid down finally, and also the educational and medical support that were required (Bürli, 1985; Guidi, 1986).

The following measures are laid down in this law:

— the abolition of 'differential' classes (see above, p.15);
— no more grades and reports (Lunetta, 1987). Instead, a kind of personal profile has to be made, consisting of:

1 data from the state and school registers and observations that may be of importance with regard to the pupil's education;
2 data concerning the child's participation in school life; descriptions on the basis of learning processes and performance level. In this part also results are given of the obligatory assessment that takes place each three months; these results have to be reported to the parents as well. Additional activities are described here too;

— special support; in Act 517/1977 there is no mention of support teachers, but of special forms of support. The concept of special teacher became officially accepted later, in Circular 199/1979. This teacher is not assigned to an individual pupil, but is in fact available for support for the whole school (Bürli, 1985).

Act 270/1982 provides the key to the number of support teachers that has to be decided annually. A school is entitled to one support teacher per two handicapped pupils in the case of severe handicaps (such as Down's syndrome or severe psycho-motor disturbances) and to one support teacher per four moderate or mildly handicapped children (mild hearing impairment, paraplegia). Support teachers in pre-school education work 30 hours a week, in primary education 24 hours and at the comprehensive school 18 hours a week (Lunetta, 1987);

— activities in small groups with a flexible structure and new manuals for the most important subjects (ibid.);

— the social–psychological–pedagogical team; at first, this was organised by the municipalities, later by the USL (organisation of local health services) (Guidi, 1986). The USLs were established by Act 833/1978 (Lunetta, 1987). Support services (services for social welfare, health and school guidance) for special education fall under the Department of Public Health. These services are administered regionally. In the sixties, the medical profession got a place in education, initially to give vaccinations and examine pupils with behavioural problems. In the late sixties psychologists and pedagogues were also appointed by the local health care services. In so-called psycho-pedagogical groups they gave information to teachers. At present, support is provided by multi-disciplinary teams that usually consist of psychologists, speech therapists and education officers. Besides, the class assistant is an important aid in regular classes (Bürli, 1985);

— the replacement of the term 'handicapped' by 'portatori di handicap' ('carrier' of a handicap). This is an essential distinction, for the latter concept no longer refers to the whole person (Lunetta, 1987).

After Act 517/1977 many other laws and ministerial circulars followed, issued by the 'Ufficio speciale per i problemi degli alluni handicappati', by which the realisation of integration was supported: in Circular 169/1978 total integration was advocated again, while attention was also drawn to the need to take account in education of the specific requirements of each individual and class; in Circular 258/1983 the emphasis was laid on co-operation between schools, local authorities and local health centres with regard to the care of handicapped pupils. It is deemed particularly important that measures are taken in time in order to prevent poor adaptation and segregation. Yearly, an educational programme has to be drawn up for the handicapped pupil by the teacher. Circular 250/1985 goes deeper into this matter. It refers to a 'functional diagnosis' which, through extensive collaboration between the parties involved (local health centres, school, pupil, parents), should result in an individualised educational programme, which has to be carefully integrated into the total educational programme.

The functional diagnosis has to reveal the principal areas of deficiency and developmental potential, so that a selection of appropriate educational measures will be possible. In carrying out the educational programme that has thus come about, the method of gradual progression has to be followed (working up to inter-mediate goals) and use has to be made of a variety of methods and instruments. The joint responsibility of all the teachers for all the handicapped pupils in the school is stressed.

Concerning integration in non-compulsory education the High Court Sentence 215 of June 1987 should be mentioned. Through this Sentence the right of integrated education is extended to higher education. It should be clear however that integration in higher education is proceeding very slowly (Ferro, 1992). Finally, we should mention the recent Reform Act 104, February 1992, covering 'welfare, social integration and rights of handicapped persons'. In this Act an attempt is made to complete, to structure and to confirm former legislation on school integration (ibid.).

The organisation of special education

Since the seventies a large proportion of the pupils of special schools and classes have been integrated into regular education, and there are only a few schools for separate special education left. These are mainly schools and institutes for the blind, the deaf and severely mentally or physically handicapped children. Statistics show a clear decrease in the number of schools for special educa-tion and the number of handicapped pupils in special education in the last decades (Eurydice, 1983; Ministero della Pubblica Istru-zione, 1985, 1990). At the same time, the number of children with special needs in regular education has increased.

Table 2.1 gives an overview of the number of handicapped children in different levels of regular education over several years. As can be seen from this table, the total percentage of handicapped pupils integrated into regular education has been increasing up to 1990.

The identification and assessment of special needs are con-ducted by paediatricians or multi-disciplinary teams consisting of

Table 2.1 Percentages of handicapped pupils in regular education in Italy (number of handicapped children as a percentage of the total school population)

Year	Pre-school	Elementary	Lower secondary	Total
1979	0.7	1.5	0.6	1.1
1985	0.7	1.7	1.5	1.5
1990	0.8	1.8	2.0	1.7

Source: Ministero della Pubblica Istruzione, 1985 and 1990

a doctor, a psychologist and a social worker. In order to receive the statutory special help in a regular class, a child should be registered as handicapped ('certificazione'). In the certificate (which is valid for one year, after which a decision on continuation or cancellation should take place) the extent to which support is needed has to be specified.

Parents have the right to be consulted on the educational provision for their children. If they do not want the child to be registered, the school does not receive extra facilities for the child (registration can only take place with the parents' approval) (Bowman, Wedell and Wedell, 1985). In practice this sometimes leads to problems for teachers who are deprived of extra assistance because parents or psychologists refuse to have the child registered. Registered children are entitled to a varying extent of support education per week. The average ratio of support teacher to number of pupils is now about 1:2.7 (Ferro, 1992).

INTEGRATION

It can be concluded that the integration principle in Italy has become a national reality. Parents and society at large seem to have accepted integration as an important educational goal. About 99 per cent of all children with special needs have been integrated into regular education by now (Lunetta, 1987). Integration is most advanced in Florence, Bologna, Trieste and Parma (Bürli, 1985; Hegarty, Pocklington and Lucas, 1981; Thannhäuser, 1983), where also the most severely handicapped have access to regular classes.

There has been a quantitative increase in integration, as the statistics show, but of course the integration process has encountered some difficulties. At the beginning of the eighties,

Galliani (1982) and others concluded that, although the integration of pupils with special needs developed, there were still problems to be solved.

For example, the number of state schools for special education declined, but there was also an increase in the number of mentally and sensorily handicapped pupils in private schools for special education, which might be indicative of problems with integration in regular schools (Bowman, Wedell and Wedell, 1985). Furthermore, it would not be correct to speak of a harmonious and continuous development of the integration process. There are large regional differences with regard to integration policy and the practical realisation of integration (Bürli, 1985; Lunetta, 1987). The coordination of integration at the central level is minimal. Moreover, the help pupils finally receive appears to be highly dependent on the support and facilities that happen to have been assigned to their region, the amount of which can vary substantially from region to region, dependent in turn on the political climate and social and economic factors (Lunetta, 1987). Recently, in 1990, a permanent inter-ministerial office (Osservatorio Permanente) was established in order to monitor practice, to coordinate policies and to advise the government. Through this office efforts are made to maximise central coordination.

At the beginning of the last decade Roser found that most teachers did not reject integration but that they encountered serious problems in implementing it in classroom practice (Roser, 1981). He reported that teachers felt relieved when they could pass the responsibility for the education of the handicapped children on to the support teachers. Teachers preferred the support teacher to work with the child outside the classroom.

Other authors also describe problems concerning integration. Lunetta (1987), for instance, distinguishes respectively 'integration in the class', 'integration outside the class' and 'wild integration'. The latter especially occurred in the first years following the implementation of Act 517/1977; the handicapped child was included in a class after which it was left alone. This resulted in a kind of isolation process, which can still be found.

Though a lot of problems were encountered in the process of integration, practice has indicated that there was often a willingness to work on integration and that finally people were looking for solutions.

In the literature various reasons are brought forward to explain why the implementation of integration in Italy has these problems. In the first place the integration process was started without investigating the needs in the regions, nor had there been an examination of which structures existed and which experts were available (Galliani, 1982).

Secondly, teacher training is limited with respect to integration. Regular teachers often do not know what to do with handicapped pupils (Bürli, 1985; Galliani, 1982; OECD, 1985). The in-service training programme (varying from two or three days to a month) did not lead to improvement, and a lot of teachers did not attend the training (Bürli, 1985; Galliani, 1982). The support teachers have made less contribution to integration than expected. In many cases these teachers cannot cope with handicapped children (Galliani, 1982; OECD, 1985). Furthermore, co-operation between the class teacher and the support teacher is often problematic. Often, the class teacher passes the education of these pupils completely on to the support teacher. It also occurs that the support teachers are charged with the care of socio-culturally deprived pupils, because the latter offer more problems to the class teacher than do mentally or physically handicapped children (Lunetta, 1987).

A final problem that should be mentioned relates to severely handicapped children. Some people want to reintroduce special classes for this group of pupils. However, this proposal is rejected in principle, because it might lead to a new separate system of special education for all weaker pupils, since it is difficult to draw a line between the different degrees of handicap (Bürli, 1985). Besides, a reintroduction of separate classes and schools is rejected, because they have proved to be discriminatory in the past and without pedagogical use (Lunetta, 1987).

A matter to be discussed separately is the comprehensive secondary school, where the willingness to handle pupils with special needs is limited and the materials for the education of these pupils are insufficient. Some teachers do not consider it their task to educate handicapped pupils (Kropveld, 1983) and also parents of non-handicapped children sometimes object to the presence of handicapped pupils in the regular class. The teachers were badly prepared for the integration of handicapped children (Ministero della Pubblica Istruzione, 1990). Accusations are also made in the direction of the primary school, where too much emphasis is laid on socialisation and too little on knowledge, resulting in knowledge gaps (Bürli, 1985).

Most of the support teachers in the comprehensive school have had no special training (Ministero della Pubblica Istruzione, 1985). They mainly work separately with the handicapped pupils, while the subject teachers instruct in a traditional teacher-centred way and 'tolerate' the presence of the handicapped pupils and the 'disturbance' they cause. Also at this level of education the co-operation between subject teacher and support teacher leaves much to be desired (Bürli, 1985).

In summary, Italy strongly advocates integration but through a lack of systematic central evaluation, little is known of the effects of the integration policy. Although the virtually complete integration of pupils with special needs seems to have been accomplished, the question remains to what degree Italy has achieved social or curricular integration. Nevertheless, integration as a goal seems to have been accepted on a large scale.

3

DENMARK

Sip Jan Pijl

INTRODUCTION

A characteristic feature of the Danish educational system is its high degree of decentralisation. Accordingly, legislation and regulations are put in place only when it is felt that they are relevant to the situation of local authorities: central government follows local developments and confines itself to drawing up general laws, which can be developed further at local level.

This same pattern can be found in the integration of regular and special education in Denmark. Before the turn of the century a number of municipalities educated mildly handicapped children within regular education. This development has continued: an increasing number of municipalities became involved in this integration process and included within it children with other handicapping conditions. In 1969, the Danish parliament decided that integration should be one of the basic principles in the education of students with special needs.

The goal of integration was closely linked to the goal of normalisation, that is, to have handicapped young people grow up in their own environment as much as possible and to ensure that special education intrudes on their lives as little as possible. The education of pupils with special needs has to start from the individual pupil's needs and – a further aspect of normalisation – has to be aimed at the objectives that apply to the regular school. The three concepts mentioned above, decentralisation, integration and normalisation, have been central to the development of the education of pupils with special needs (Magne, 1987).

THE EDUCATIONAL SYSTEM

Structure

The educational system of Denmark is very much aimed at creating possibilities for the integration of different groups in society: children from different social classes, children with special needs and children from other ethnic groups. As a consequence, the education is hardly split up: the large majority of children attend the public school, the so-called Folkeskole.

Pre-school provision for the 0–7-year-olds is made in day nurseries, pre-school kindergartens and the pre-school classes of the Folkeskole. The first two types of provision are administered by the Ministry of Social Affairs (Eurydice, 1986).

Approximately 35 per cent of children between 0 and 5 years attend a day nursery or a pre-school kindergarten; there are more older than younger children who attend a form of pre-school education, ranging from 35 to 90 per cent. About 90 per cent of children attend the pre-school classes of the Folkeskole (Eurydice, 1986). Pre-school education is not completely financed by the (local) authorities; parents, depending on their income, contribute about 35 per cent of the costs (Bürli, 1985).

Children receive their education at the Folkeskole, which is free of charge, or go to private schools. The latter are financed, and thus administered, up to 85 per cent by the central government while the remainder is covered by school fees (Eurydice, 1986). The Folkeskole consists of the pre-school classes for 6–7-year-olds, the Grundskole for 7–16-year-olds and a tenth, optional year, which serves as a preparatory course for a few types of secondary education. Education is compulsory for children from 7 to 16 years (Danish Ministry of Education, 1991b). The pre-school classes offer a preparation for the Grundskole. Since 1986, children from the pre-school classes in small schools follow joint lessons with the lower two classes of the Grundskole, except for the subjects Danish and arithmetic (Eurydice, 1986).

The Grundskole comprises primary and lower secondary education. In the first seven years all students follow the same programme within one school; differences can exist between schools. Especially from the eighth grade on, a large variety of non-compulsory subjects can be offered. During the whole period in the Grundskole, children stay in the same class group.

In the Act on the Folkeskole of 1990 (Danish Ministry of Education, 1991b), the national government has made, in addition to the core subjects, seven topics compulsory, such as traffic safety, Norwegian and Swedish, new information technology. In addition, each municipality has the right to add compulsory topics. There are also a number of non-compulsory subjects that every school should offer in principle, for example German. From the eighth grade, the elementary subjects can be offered at two levels (Eurydice, 1986), although this does not often happen. There is a tendency to keep the whole group of pupils at the same level. Doubts about the level of the Folkeskole may be partly responsible for an increase in the number of private schools in the past decade. It is possible, however, for parents to insist that a differentiation into two levels is carried through in the Folkeskole.

Pupils and parents are regularly informed about pupils' performance. At least twice a year an account is given of the pupil's performance, social behaviour and strong and weak points. Mostly, this information is communicated orally, but from the eighth grade, written reports, in which performance is expressed in marks, are given. At the end of the Folkeskole, pupils receive a 'leaving' certificate which details their performance in the different subjects. At their own request, pupils may sit for a leaving examination or an advanced examination.

The number of pupils in a class in the Folkeskole must be no higher than twenty-eight; the current average is approximately nineteen. In principle, the education and support of a class in the Grundskole are the responsibility of the same teacher throughout the entire school period. The number of lessons per week varies from fifteen to eighteen for the youngest children to twenty-eight to thirty-four for the higher grades (Danish Ministry of Education, 1991b). The educational facilities of the Folkeskole are highly differentiated and offer instructional possibilities for pupils with a wide range of problems. A team-teaching model is often used. The schools are free to choose teaching methods and materials.

Legislation, administration and policy

The recent history of Denmark is characterised by great social care for its inhabitants. This care is also reflected in the present educational system and its administrative form. In the past few decades the organisation of the educational system and its administrative forms have been underpinned by three concepts (Danish Ministry of Education, 1992):

— normalisation: the challenge to society to allow handicapped people to lead a life that is as normal as possible;
— integration: the effort to treat handicapped and non-handicapped people in the same way and to remove the special position of the handicapped;
— decentralisation/regionalisation: the effort to bring public services and power of decision as near as possible to the people; in practice to the municipality or the county.

Since the sixties, Danish society has been organised in such a way that these three principles have been met. Laws have been enacted and measures have been taken that promote the normalisation and integration of handicapped people, such as the foundation of the Folkeskole. The principle of decentralisation has resulted in a larger power of decision for municipalities and counties with regard to education, within Government guidelines (Bürli, 1985; Döbrich *et al.*, 1984; Hansen, 1992).

Responsibility for Danish education is spread in various ways among the central authorities, the counties, the municipalities, committees and individual persons (Danish Ministry of Education, 1983). Parliament determines the goals for the different types of education and decides how financial resources are divided between them.

The Ministry of Education carries the final responsibility for education. It consists of six directorates that are each responsible for a section of education. The Ministry has the following administrative tasks:

— setting targets for each subject;
— drawing up and issuing ministerial ordinances and circulars, giving curriculum guidelines and making recommendations;
— general supervision;
— appeal in cases relating to salary and appointment of teachers;
— allocation of (minor) block grants for education to municipalities.

28

The regional authorities are responsible for the entire education in one region and in particular for the gymnasia, higher preparatory courses, adult education and for special education. It should be noted that the county administers special education in co-operation with the municipalities in which they are located. The region approves and supervises the measures taken by the municipalities. In fact, educational administration lies with the regional councils, which consist of a number of elected members.

The municipality councils are also elected. They administer and have overall responsibility for the actual state of affairs in the local school system. The regular schools are financed by the municipalities and through a minor block grant from the state to the municipalities. The municipal authorities can delegate parts of their power to the school boards. Each school has a school board. It consists of five to seven elected members: parents/guardians, a municipality representative, two teachers and two pupils. If special classes are attached to the school, parents of pupils from these classes should be represented as well.

The head teacher has the overall administrative and pedagogical responsibility for the school. The head teacher puts into effect the board's policy guidelines, allocates duties to all staff members and makes all important decisions regarding pupils (Danish Ministry of Education, 1991c).

Private schools can be founded by a group of parents who have special educational, political or religious convictions. Private schools are subsidised and controlled up to 85 per cent by the state: the education in these schools has to meet the requirements that also apply to the Folkeskole. Each school has to draw up an educational programme, which sets out the content and organisation of education in that school.

SPECIAL NEEDS EDUCATION

Developments in special education

In the nineteenth century, a beginning was made with the care for the handicapped, which mainly functioned on the basis of initiatives by private institutions. This resulted in a large number of institutions for the handicapped in the twenties. In 1933, the government took over financial responsibility for the treatment of handicapped people and reorganised the institutions. During the decade 1950–60, the government was active in normalising the position of the mentally handicapped in particular, who up till then had been looked after in big nursing homes, isolated from society. This led to the passing of a law in 1959, in which compulsory attendance was mandated (this already existed for other handicapped people) and which laid down the rules for proper educational facilities. Since that time, all handicapped people have been entitled to education.

Since the sixties, experience has been gained in the integration of children with special needs into regular education, and special teachers have worked in regular schools. The strongest motives for the trend towards integration were parents' wishes and the acceptance of pedagogical theories about the positive aspects of integration. One of the first attempts was the establishment of special classes in regular schools, the so-called centre classes, for pupils with more severe handicaps, such as visual, hearing and motor disabilities. At the same time a growing number of blind children were enrolled separately – due to their small number – in regular classes. Both centre classes and individual integration were experienced as feasible and appropriate solutions (Hansen, 1992). In 1969, the parliament decided that children with special needs should be educated as far as possible in a normal school environment; this was confirmed by the Act on the Folkeskole (1975), which came into force 1 January 1980. In 1972 a special task force was established which, among other things, had to make proposals for a coherent system of regular and special education. These proposals were laid down by law in 1980 (Bürli, 1985). They describe, for instance, what is meant by special educational assistance for pupils: (1) special instruction; (2) stimulation and training (e. g. of sensory or physical functions); (3) counselling and support (of parents, teachers); (4) educational aids; and (5) personal assistance (Danish Ministry of Education, 1988a, 1991d).

In view of the principle of regionalisation, the administration of special education should differ as little as possible from regular education. Moreover, according to the principle of normalisation, special provision for pupils should be realised as much as possible in the regular setting (Danish Ministry of Education, 1991b). Responsibility for the support of the relatively mildly handicapped therefore rests with the municipalities, who have to provide special education facilities in the Folkeskole (Act on the Folkeskole, 1990, section 19.1). The municipalities have to provide not only special education but also special educational support for children who are not yet of school age. In addition, they carry the responsibility for education in hospitals and other institutions within the municipality. The transport of handicapped and sick pupils is also one of the tasks of the municipality. The municipality has to set out its policy regarding special education in a plan for the county.

The county (the next level of administration) is responsible for the education of pupils 'whose development calls for special extensive consideration or support' (Act on the Folkeskole, 1990, section 19.2).

Referral to any form of special instruction should be based on an educational/psychological examination of the child and consultation with the parents (Danish Ministry of Education, 1991b).

The organisation of special education

Denmark no longer has a separate system of special education, but rather a continuum of types of education varying from regular to highly specialised, a major part of which is closely connected to the regular schools. Note that the concept 'Folkeskole' contains both. Regular and special education fall within the same legislative arrangements and have the same educational goals and means. Table 3.1 offers an overview of the educational possibilities for pupils with special needs.

From the range of possibilities shown in Table 3.1, it can be seen that there are several forms of integration in Danish education. Groups of pupils with special needs may receive only part of their education in one or a few subjects as special education, while in the 'clinic' they receive all of their education in one or more subjects in the form of special education. Many special education schools have been incorporated into regular schools in the past few years. Not only buildings and classrooms but also the educational offerings have become part of the regular schools. The great majority of children attend a Folkeskole or a private school without needing special help. The major proportion of the other pupils, who do need extra support, receive special pedagogical help that is linked to the regular class.

Physically handicapped pupils who, apart from the specific

Table 3.1 Educational facilities for pupils with special needs in Denmark

Regular school with one extra teacher	One person in charge of the teaching	Special groups established in connection with a normal school	Clinic of special education at normal school	Special class established at the child's local school	Special class at a normal school outside the local school district	Special school department established in connection with a normal school (twin school)	Special school	Special boarding school or residential institution

Source: Danish Ministry of Education (1991d)

problems caused by their handicap, do not have further problems with their school work, follow the regular programme and receive special support for a number of hours per week. This method is used also for blind children and some mentally handicapped children. The support consists, for instance, of learning to work with teaching aids and materials in relation to the regular education programme that is being followed by the whole class, of speech and/or physiotherapy and of support with care requirement.

Pupils who have problems in one or more subjects are taught in these subjects in 'groups', part-time or full-time, usually by a special teacher; this refers mostly to basic subjects such as arithmetic and native language education. Nowadays, the majority of children with serious problems do not go to a 'group', but to a 'clinic'. A clinic consists of a classroom which is equipped with remedial education materials. The lessons are provided by a special teacher. Children with behavioural problems, or children with problems in (one of) the basic subjects, are taught in the clinic while their own class is having these subjects (Bürli, 1985). Also, children who attend the higher classes of the Folkeskole can be taught in the clinic, for example, if they have problems with a particular teacher. In this way, socio-psychological tension is prevented.

In the special class of the Folkeskole, pupils are taught in all the subjects. The support in special classes is mainly directed at pupils with learning problems, but also hearing impaired pupils and pupils with physical handicaps can be helped there. As a rule, there are no special classes for children with learning problems in the first and second grade (Bürli, 1985). Moreover, the aim of education is to return children who have been placed in a special class to the regular class. Special classes cater for children who have attended separate special schools. There are still special schools, but some of these have recently been closed and other special schools have been transformed into special classes in regular schools. Also, municipalities themselves take the initiative to establish a special class in one of the regular schools. It is as yet unknown to what extent social or curricular integration is achieved for pupils in a special class.

Finally, pupils have the possibility of following a 'reading course': over a period of time which may not be longer than six months, they are taught intensively in those subjects that have been directly affected by serious reading problems.

Within the 'Folkeskole' system, there are some other institutions in which special education takes place. In 'observation' schools, children with behavioural problems are observed and educated. Observation schools are boarding schools in which the children are placed for a short period, with the agreement of their parents.

'Centres for special education' are intended for relatively severely handicapped children. These centres are spread all over the country and cater for children from a certain region within a radius of about 50 kilometres; the distance from school to home is such that the children can go home daily. The centres are connected to a regular school and offer the full range of classes from the first to the ninth form. Schools can have a centre (in fact one or more special education classes) for children with a certain handicap or for children with different sorts of handicaps. The centres for special education have partly taken over the educational tasks carried out by special schools.

Table 3.2 shows the number of children in the different types of special education in the year 1986/7 (these are the most recent data available). The Danish Ministry of Education considers that these figures represent the present situation reasonably accurately, given that the overall decline in number of children results in lower frequencies and that the ongoing closing down of special schools should result in a slightly lower percentage for the special schools and a slightly higher one for the special classes.

Currently, there are thirty-four schools for special education in Denmark, twenty-six of which are for mentally handicapped pupils, three for deaf pupils and one school each for the blind, the physically handicapped, epileptic, dyslexic and autistic children. These schools have many facilities for dealing with the specific types of handicaps. Depending on the type of special education, they employ psychologists, speech therapists, physiotherapists and doctors. One school for speech disorders also offers adult education and there is a special division for children with a cleft palate.

Finally, there are peripatetic remedial educationalists who give assistance to visually or auditorily handicapped children, children with speech disorders and children with behavioural problems (Bürli, 1985).

In the year 1990 approximately 80,000 pupils received some form of special education. This is 12.5 per cent of the total number of pupils, a percentage which has remained fairly constant over the

Table 3.2 Number of children in the different types of special education in Denmark in the year 1986/7 and as a percentage of the total population*

Year 1986/7	Number	%
Special education connected to normal class education:		
in class	12,451	1.97
clinic/team	45,977	7.28
individual	10,387	1.64
Special education *not* connected to normal class education:		
special class at normal school	6,033	0.96
special school: municipal	1,258	0.20
county	2,378	0.38
individual	418	0.07
Observation school	527	0.08
Total	79,429	12.57
Other kind of special pedagogic assistance	4,083	0.65

Source: Danish Ministry of Education (1988b).
* Most recent statistics available in 1992.

past few years. The participation was highest among the age group 9–13 years. The majority of pupils receiving special education are placed in a clinic at a regular school, as can be seen in Table 3.2.

Referral and placement

According to section 11(2) of the Act on the Folkeskole, a child with problems of any kind can be referred to a form of special education on the basis of a school psychological examination and after consultation with the parents and, if desired, with the child (Danish Ministry of Education, 1991b).

For the support and referral of children with problems there are school psychological services, where educational psychologists, special teachers, clinical psychologists and social workers are employed. There are also consultants or advisers for problems in specific areas, such as speech and hearing disorders and problems concerning choice of career.

When in practice problems with a pupil have been observed, the teacher contacts the school psychological service. To begin with, the child is examined by an educational psychologist and – depending on the nature and the severity of the problems – also by experts from other disciplines. Based on this examination, an educational programme is drawn up in consultation with the teacher and, if necessary, with the special teacher and the parents. The programme is carried out by either the regular or the special teacher. It can vary from extra support in the classroom to segregated special education. In time, the programme can be adapted after evaluation of its effect (Jørgensen, 1979). Bürli (1985) notes, however, that in practice written educational programmes are seldom used.

INTEGRATION

The efforts to achieve integration are directly linked to the pursuit of 'normalisation'; that is to allow handicapped people to lead a life that is as normal as possible and to minimise the intrusion of special education in their lives.

As a result, the regular school caters for most of the schooling of pupils with problems. The support of mildly handicapped pupils is the responsibility of the municipality, which has to provide special education facilities within the regular school (section 19.1 of the Act). The region is responsible for the more severely handicapped pupils (section 19.2 of the Act). Besides the regular school, a number of other options for special education exist, as we have described above. The way in which the integration of regular and special education is realised in Denmark can be described on the basis of the division of Bruun and Koefoed (1982, p. 13). They distinguish four levels of integration, namely: the regular and special school as twin schools, the regular school with a special class or with a few special classes (centre classes), the regular school with a 'clinic' and integrated education.

By setting up twin schools (two separate schools that co-operate on a limited scale) a certain degree of social integration is aimed at (Magne, 1987). As for the possibilities for integration, the next variant, the Folkeskole with one or more special classes, resembles the twin schools. In this variant special and regular education are provided under the same roof, but the possibilities for integration are limited to social integration. How much of this is realised in practice strongly depends on the situation. If it concerns one special class in a school, e.g. for pupils with learning difficulties, social integration will be feasible. In the case of a few special classes (centre classes) for mentally handicapped pupils, for instance, even this is not always an explicit aim. In that case the special classes mainly operate as separate units to give the group of pupils concerned a chance for personal development. Accordingly, these groups organise project weeks, holidays and sports days separately from the regular group. The desire of handicapped pupils to be educated together is taken very seriously in special education in Denmark. Research has shown that, among others, hard-of-hearing pupils in regular classes prefer to be in small classes with other hard-of-hearing pupils. Nowadays they are educated as far as possible in small units in the Folkeskole that are specialised in their type of handicap. In other words, a special class is created deliberately (Lau, personal communication, 1988).

The regular school with a clinic has been the pivot of the integration process for a long time. In principle, each regular school has a clinic or has ready access to one in the neighbourhood. By means of the clinic it is intended to place all the available knowledge on special education and special education materials at the disposal of pupils within the regular school. Pupils can attend the clinic for one or more subjects whilst their own class is also engaged in the subject(s) concerned. The problem here is that special education in that subject, for instance 'language', takes so much more time than in regular education, that all the attractive, relaxing activities around this subject have to be cancelled. As a result, 'language' in the clinic is reduced to, for example, reading and spelling instruction only. Besides, it has been found that pupils stay dependent on instruction in the clinic for much too long. In order to avoid these disadvantages, the so-called intensive course is used more frequently nowadays, in particular for children with learning problems. For three to six months the pupil has ten to fifteen lessons weekly in the subject causing difficulty. The first experiences are positive: there is a strong reduction in learning problems and pupils need special education for a considerably shorter period

(Lau, personal communication, 1988). In order to prevent the possible recurrence of difficulties, a combination of intensive course and clinic is also used.

Education in the group and individual education, both in the regular class, are regarded as integrated education. In both variants pupils with special needs stay in their own class and receive extra assistance for part of the time, in small groups or individually. For this extra support an itinerant teacher for special education, for example a 'reading consultant', can visit the school. Apart from giving specific support to the pupil, the itinerant teacher's task consists of advising the teacher.

It is clear that the special help for pupils with problems in this model comes nearest to what Kobi (1983) calls curricular integration.

DISCUSSION

Danish education is considered by many as pioneering and progressive because of its far-reaching integration of regular and special education, and has been widely used as an example (Magne, 1987). Although decentralisation makes it difficult to achieve a detailed understanding of the local elaboration of plans and measures, it is clear that through a resolute and pragmatic approach the integration of special and regular education has reached an advanced stage in Denmark.

Blake (1984) mentions two possible reasons for this success. She points out that Danish society is fairly homogeneous in social, cultural and financial respects. This enhances the acceptance of pupils with special needs by 'normal' pupils and teachers, which makes integration more attainable. The second reason has to do with the organisation of the educational system. In Danish schools teachers stay with their classes throughout the whole school period. In principle, the three subject teachers (of reading and language, arithmetic and the creative subjects) accompany their pupils from grade one through into secondary education. In this way teachers come to know their pupils very well (and vice versa) and develop a greater involvement with and responsibility for them: after all, in this system the teacher also will 'suffer' for years from a badly tackled learning problem. Jansen (personal communication, 1988) adds another characteristic of Danish education that may be relevant here. Danish education is characterised by a relaxed atmosphere, which improves the school climate and frees many pupils from the pressure to perform. It can also lead, however, to a creeping inflation of instructional goals and performances.

The final aspect of Danish integration that should be mentioned is the high number of pupils receiving some form of special education during their school career. It is estimated that 25 per cent of all the pupils sooner or later, for a shorter or a longer period, get special education (Danish Ministry of Education, 1991d). If one out of four pupils receives special education at some point in their school career, it can hardly be called special any longer.

In summary, special education in separate schools/classes is not and will not be abolished in Denmark. Measures are taken, however, to realise a certain degree of social integration. A whole range of integration alternatives have been developed for pupils who are able to follow special education in more integrated settings. Making use of these special facilities has become very normal.

4

SWEDEN

Sip Jan Pijl

INTRODUCTION

In the past decades, the Swedish educational system has undergone dramatic changes. In the early fifties most pupils received education for no more than six or seven years (while almost 100 per cent now attend school for at least eleven years) and the education on offer was out of date. Less than 5 per cent of the population attained the higher levels of education (polytechnics and universities). Only 10 per cent completed secondary education (Gran, 1986).

Substantive school reforms began in the fifties. In 1950 the parliament decided to introduce a nine-year compulsory and comprehensive school. In the years following, experiments with this new type of school took place to an increasing extent. In 1962 there were more experimental than there were 'old' schools, which made it easy for the parliament to implement the so-called Grundskola definitively. After 1962, the number of pupils receiving a form of special education grew rapidly. At first this development was accepted, but in a few years the costs doubled. Also the segregation of a growing number of students became a problem from a political point of view.

Educational policy in Sweden is strongly influenced by the social democratic ideology, in which equality of opportunity is one of the central issues. This so-called Myrdal trend is aimed at a just division of wealth, health care, work, education, housing, food, leisure and so forth, in such a way that individuals have the opportunity to develop their talents to the full and are able to live actively in society (see Magne, 1987). From this point of view, the

41

placement in separate schools of deviant pupils and/or those who cannot keep up with their peers is highly undesirable.

This political ideology, as well as the growing pressure of voluntary bodies to enable handicapped pupils to participate fully in education, the relatively high costs of special education, plus the fact that the number receiving special education went up rapidly, all contributed to the integration advice of the SIA committee (Skolans Inre Arbete, established in 1975). This advice was incorporated in the LGR 80 (Läroplan för Grundskolan), the new curriculum for primary and lower secondary education, which was published in 1980 and came into force in 1983.

THE EDUCATIONAL SYSTEM

Structure

Since 1962, Sweden has had a uniform system of education, compulsory for children aged between 7 and 16. Virtually all educational provision for children from 7 to 19 years is centrally controlled (Eklindh, 1985).

Pre-school care for children from 0 to 7 years takes place in day nurseries and pre-school kindergartens. Pre-school education is not compulsory, but the municipalities have the duty to secure that arrangements are made for pre-school education for 6-year-olds (Eklindh, 1985). Pre-school education can be full-time or part-time. In 1984, 92,308 6-year-olds attended a kindergarten (98.5 per cent of the age population), of whom two-thirds were part-time and one-third full-time. In the same year, 47.8 per cent of the 5-year-olds went to a kindergarten, a relatively low percentage due to a shortage of places.

Compulsory education is divided into three levels: junior (grades one to three), intermediate (grades four to six) and senior (grades seven to nine) (Eklindh, 1985). The schools are split up into working units (*arbetsenheter*), consisting of three to four classes of approximately the same level. Within a working unit pupils can be grouped in different ways, so that methods and – depending on the educational subject – level can be adapted as far as possible to the pupils' individual abilities and capacities. The centre of a working unit is a team, usually consisting of the teachers from the different classes, a special teacher, and sometimes a school psychologist or a social worker. It should be noted that the special education teacher is added to the working unit, even if there are no registered pupils with special needs in it. The working unit operates according to the team-teaching model (Eklindh, 1985; Söder, 1984; Swedish National Board of Education, 1985). In principle, the members of a working unit share the responsibility for the educational provision made. Through this way of organisation, the Swedish educational system offers a wide range of facilities for pupils with special needs, which is in accordance with the national policy that is aimed at care for the handicapped and social integration (Eklindh, 1985). Less than 1 per cent of all pupils attend a separate school for special education (Statistiska Centralbyrån, 1986).

Higher secondary education is provided by institutes that offer more than twenty different courses in three areas: arts and the social sciences; economic and commercial subjects; the natural sciences and technical subjects. Courses last for two, three or sometimes four years; they may be followed by additional courses, usually professional training (OECD, 1980).

Legislation, administration and policy

The original school system in Sweden was based on the old academic schools dating from the Middle Ages, built and maintained by the Catholic Church. After the Reformation in the sixteenth century, these came under the control of the government. The local authorities financed the buildings, and the government financed teachers' salaries and educational materials.

By law dating from 1842, schools for all children, compulsory schools, were to be built in all parishes, which were the original municipalities in Sweden. A parallel school system (the original state schools, for upper-class children and children from the countryside who wanted to enter the church, and the compulsory schools) continued until 1927. From that date, all pupils had to spend four to six years in the compulsory school (OECD, 1979). In 1940, education was compulsory for about six years and only 10 per cent of the pupils completed secondary education. There were very few schools for special education.

When the major school reforms began, the old medieval parishes (some 2,000) were combined into new, larger local municipalities

(278 in 1952) (OECD, 1979). Since the fifties, far-reaching innovations have been implemented in the educational system, aimed at raising the general level of education. At the same time a growing need was felt to create equal opportunities for everybody. From 1962, the parallel school system was abandoned altogether and the compulsory and comprehensive nine-year school, the Grundskola, was introduced, which is open to every pupil. In 1962 the Education Act was passed, which provided the basic regulations for this school system. It laid down the duration of compulsory schooling (from 7 to 16), the division of the elementary school into nine grades, the organisation of the school health services, the institution in every municipality of a local education authority (LEA), and so forth (OECD, 1979).

From 1962, the public Grundskola became the only form of education for children aged between 7 and 16 in Sweden (Grundin, 1979; OECD, 1979, 1981a). In 1983, this Act was replaced by its successor, the LGR 80 (Läroplan för Grundskolan).

Because of the effort to achieve equality between pupils, differentiation is avoided as much as possible within regular education. Education is aimed at maximum integration and, through that, normalisation of handicapped pupils. Although differentiation is avoided, a strong emphasis is placed on individualisation, which is manifested in the large variety of special instructional facilities, in which integration of special and regular education is stressed. This means an emphasis on individualisation within the class or working unit. Recent policy initiatives are meant to enhance the integration process by raising the level of teacher training for both regular and special teachers, by putting in special teachers as consultants in regular education and by supporting experimental projects in which a curriculum is being developed for all pupils in the school (the so-called 'Skolans för alla' project).

The structure of educational administration in Sweden is strongly related to the integration objectives mentioned above. Until recently, Sweden had always been a highly centrally governed state. The financial reason for close state control was complemented by an ideological reason: the desire to give the same opportunity for education to all pupils irrespective of the type of municipality in which they lived (OECD, 1979). After a few years, however, decentralisation and the need for more civil involvement led to a delegation of administrative government responsibilities to local and regional authorities. The elementary schools and the schools for higher secondary education are now administered and, since July 1991, also financed by the local authorities, whereas legislation is a matter of central government.

Immediately subordinate to the government (the Ministry of Education), are three central administrative boards, covering different fields of administration, namely the National Agency for Schools, the National Agency for Special Education and the National Board for Universities and Polytechnics. These boards evaluate, inspect and provide advice and guidance to the educational system; they draw up curricula, distribute funds for research and provide counselling services in special education.

At the local level, the municipal or local education authority, consisting of elected politicians, carries the full responsibility for educational planning, for matters concerning the content of educational subjects, and for practical matters such as school meals and pupil transport, all within the boundaries of governmental legislation. The local authorities are authorised to make their own decisions in matters that are not centrally regulated. Some responsibilities are delegated to the head teachers of the separate schools (Eklindh, 1985; OECD, 1981a). Also the teachers of the Grundskola and the parents have a substantial say in educational matters. The teachers discuss future developments and changes in education with the local authorities and give them advice; they have, however, no power of decision. Parents can have influence on education in class meetings of parents, pupils and teachers, or by attending lessons in the class.

SPECIAL NEEDS EDUCATION

Historical developments

Until the sixties, handicapped children, that is mentally retarded children and children with physical and sensory handicaps, attended separate schools for special education (Eklindh, 1985; Söder, 1984). Children with other types of problems were educated in regular education, usually in special classes. This was related to the low population density, as a result of which children from a large area had to attend a single school (Grundin, 1979).

In the special classes of the Grundskola each child that was educationally retarded received all education from a special teacher, who should have had one extra year of training for this purpose. In practice, however, this was often not the case. Because of the reforms since 1960 and the growing financial possibilities, the facilities for special education had improved; more specialists entered the school (psychologists, social workers, etc.) and new facilities for special support emerged, such as clinics for various school subjects, in which pupils who scored low in these subjects could follow a number of lessons per week (Grundin, 1979). Particularly through the popularity of these clinics, the number of pupils in special education grew rapidly. In the seventies, up to 30 per cent of all pupils received some sort of special instruction, in special or in regular settings (Emanuelsson, personal communication, 1988; Stukat, personal communication, 1988). At first this was not regarded as a big problem: economic prosperity made it possible to finance a growing special education provision and the government overcame the arguments of the opponents of the Grundskola through a liberal policy towards special education. The opponents feared that the compulsory school with its uniform curriculum would have a strong negative effect on the level of education. They regarded special education as a means of preventing an excessive reduction of the level of educational achievement. But after only a few years, this development was deemed highly undesirable: the costs of education doubled, research showed that segregation had a number of disadvantages, organisations for the handicapped were striving for a more integrated educational system, and from the wider perspective of social democratic principles integration became the main objective.

During the educational reforms since the sixties, which were aimed at providing equal educational opportunities for all children, the majority of the separate special schools were abolished. Today, there are special schools only for the deaf and for mentally retarded children plus a few schools for the multiply handicapped. The schools for deaf children have continued to exist, for the education of these pupils is considered to be so very different from regular education, due to the specific communication problem, that it was not thought possible to have these pupils educated in regular settings. Integration is only considered for these pupils if they are able to communicate with each other and with other people (Eklindh, 1985).

The number of special schools for mentally retarded children has decreased sharply over the past few years. A further drop in the number of separate special schools is expected, although a few schools for the severely mentally retarded will probably continue to exist. The majority of these pupils have now been placed in special classes in the Grundskola. About one-tenth of this group is individually integrated. For multiply handicapped children there are still three special schools: for deaf children who are mentally retarded, for deaf children with speech disorders and for blind children who are mentally retarded.

The other schools for special education have closed or been assigned a different function, e.g. assistance, advice and the conduct of scientific research (Söder, 1984).

Legislation

Current policy with regard to pupils with problems has resulted from the above-mentioned developments, aimed at better support of these pupils in the Grundskola. The curriculum of 1983 (LGR 80), in which this policy is described, is based on three starting points:

1 It is not the handicap itself but the problems it causes in the interaction with the outside world that should be central. The reasons for these difficulties may partly lie within the school itself, so solutions for them have to be found within the school.
2 A holistic view of the pupil with special needs should be taken. In diagnosing the pupil's problems, the child as a whole should be taken into account, not only his or her shortcomings.
3 The problems of the child should be dealt with in its own class; the organisation of the class and the school has to be flexible. Only then can integration be realised (Söder, 1984).

Swedish education is aimed at a high degree of individualisation, the main purpose of which is to make the child feel safe and happy, in and outside the school. In fact, the policy with regard to the education of pupils with special needs is a realisation of the policy towards the care for handicapped people in general in Swedish society, which is also directed at integration and solidarity.

Special education within the Grundskola has no separate administration. Schools for special education fall under direct control of the state (OECD, 1979); only the schools for the mentally retarded are administered at the regional level (Eklindh, 1985).

The organisation of special education

Special and regular education in Sweden have been integrated to such an extent that a description of special education automatically implies a description of the regular education system.

The organisation of the education of children with special needs in the Grundskola is described in the 'Education Ordinance.' Special education should be organised at the level of the working unit or the class. If necessary, separate groups may be created for the instruction of children with severe physical handicaps, children with social emotional disturbances or with other severe problems in relation to the school tasks (Eklindh, 1985). Less drastic measures are preferred, however: giving the child extra time to do work, or arranging assistance from classmates, parents or the special teacher, within the class or working unit.

If measures in the classroom are ineffective, a child may – depending on the nature of the problems – be educated part-time or full-time in a separate group. Children who have problems in one or more subjects may get instruction in these subjects in that special group, but for the other activities they remain in their own class or working unit. Children with severe physical handicaps, with severe social and emotional disturbances or with severe learning problems can be placed full-time in a special group. After referral by, for instance, the working unit, a multi-disciplinary team decides if the referred pupil is eligible for a special education group. In 1988, about 0.5 per cent of the pupils of the Grundskola attended a special education group (Pijl and Meijer, 1991).

For pupils with severe social and emotional problems, who require intensive care that cannot be provided in the regular school, there are special day schools ('skoldaghem'). Besides education, the pupils (and their parents) can also have therapy, the final objective of which is return to the Grundskola (Swedish National Board of Education, 1982). There are more than 100 day schools attended by approximately 1,000 pupils (that is about 0.1 per cent of the population aged 6–17). For pupils with extreme social and emotional problems the so-called 'paragraph 12 homes' exist. The pupils who live there (about 550) fall under the responsibility of the Ministry of Social Affairs.

There are two other forms of education for the mentally retarded: specialised schools for elementary education with classes for mildly retarded children, and (special) training schools for severely retarded children. Policy is aimed at closing the separate training schools and placing the pupils in classes that are linked to the Grundskola. Thus the retarded pupils have the opportunity to participate in joint activities with the regular school pupils (Eklindh, 1985). In this type of education much attention is paid to learning to handle special aids and to functioning in society (Swedish National Board of Education, 1985). There are also separate special schools for deaf pupils (600 pupils in five schools), in which sign language is the first and Swedish the second language.

For a small group of multiply handicapped pupils there are three special schools, each containing around fifty pupils. All the other handicapped pupils in Sweden are placed in regular education; these include the physically handicapped, the blind and partially-sighted, and the hard-of-hearing children.

Highly specialised knowledge on the education of the blind, mentally retarded, deaf and multiply physically handicapped is concentrated in four so-called 'resource centres'. These centres, which are located in Stockholm, Umeå, Örebro and Göteborg, fulfil a great number of tasks, such as: diagnosing student problems, drawing up educational plans, training children and their parents, teacher training, research, developing methods and special aids, and sending out consultants. Many pupils are placed in these centres for a short time only, so that they have the character of a special school to a minimal degree.

Referral and placement

If special measures are to be taken by the working unit, they should be based on an educational programme drawn up by the staff of the working unit. The programme should cover:

— definition of the problem;
— description of the goal;
— the method by which to attain the goal.

(Swedish National Board of Education, 1982)

The staff of the working unit decide which children will be instructed in a special group. Pupils with problems are discussed on a regular basis within the working unit, in consultation with the parents and the children themselves (ibid.). If the pupil's problems require a very specialised educational offering, the pupil is referred to a full-time special class or a special school. A multi-disciplinary team decides about the placement on the basis of a diagnostic report and an educational programme (Pijl, De Graaf and Emanuelsson, 1988). This meticulousness in referral procedures, in which nothing is done without an educational programme, has resulted from the situation in former days when pupils could be referred to a special class or school too easily and without clear criteria (Grundin, 1979).

It should be noticed, however, that many of the children concerned (deaf, mentally handicapped, etc.) have been detected long before their school period, so this procedure is seldom necessary.

INTEGRATION

In Sweden a relatively small group of pupils, about one half per cent of the population from 7 to 17 years of age, are educated in one of the schools for special education. These are pupils with severe social and emotional problems, deaf pupils, the multiply handicapped and some of the mentally handicapped pupils. All other pupils with problems are integrated into regular education or, to quote Emanuelsson (1985), not segregated. Two models can be distinguished in the way integration is organised: integration in the regular classroom and the (full-time) special class in the regular school. The special class or – in larger schools – the special classes are principally intended for pupils with mental handicaps. The responsibility for these pupils is formally in the hands of the region. Consequently, educational facilities for this group of pupils are also provided at the regional level. In practice this means that the region appoints the special teachers for this group and pays their salaries; these teachers have their own head teacher; classrooms are hired from the regular Grundskola; teaching materials and methods are acquired through other channels and so forth. It is obvious that the separate status of these special classes easily leads to 'small schools' within the Grundskola, especially in the larger schools.

Apart from the 'special class' model, integration takes place in the regular class: pupils with problems are individually integrated into the regular class. They thus fall under the responsibility of the working unit. The exact number of children receiving special education according to this integration model (from a few hours to full-time) is unknown. It is estimated that it is at least 10 per cent of all pupils (Pijl and Meijer, 1991). Teachers in the working units have at their disposal a large range of organisational options for special education. For certain subjects teachers can give extra support in the classroom, individually or in small groups, but they can also split up the class or have the pupils taught in a small group outside the classroom or in another (lower) class, etc. As a result, the 'working unit' model consists of a wide range of organisational models.

It is not quite clear how special education in a regular setting is realised in the day-to-day practice. It seems that the majority of schools are not yet successful in integrating into regular education every member of the group of pupils with problems. In a number of schools 'difficult' pupils are passed on to the special teacher, who is considered responsible for the education of this group (Eklindh, 1985; Emanuelsson, 1985). As a result, special classes emerge again within the 'working unit' model. And this can easily occur: usually, a full-time special teacher is added to a working unit of four classes and with, for instance, five or six mentally handicapped pupils it is possible to request a full-time extra teacher.

Passing on pupils to a special class is not in keeping with the central principle of education, i.e. no segregation of pupil groups. The idea is that the joint creative force of the working unit should be capable of solving the educational problems. However, it can be assumed that many teachers are not ready for this way of working. They withdraw to their own classes and call in the assistance of the special teacher for remedial teaching and/or total support outside the class. The special teachers, however, accept this situation too. Stukat (personal communication, 1988) indicates that their role is unclear and confusing. For example, on the one hand they are expected to trace and diagnose pupils' problems, on the other hand they are not allowed to label them and to make exceptions. Regular teachers expect them to provide special methods for special problems, while, in fact, these methods are difficult to transfer. In principle, they should not take children with problems out of the class, but at the same time these children should be given the opportunity to develop their own identity in contacts with other 'handicapped' students. It is also unclear who carries the responsibility for the education of pupils with problems: the special education teacher should be the moving force, but the working unit is responsible.

The tendency towards segregation of difficult pupils by the regular teacher and the difficult position of the special education teacher are important problems in the integration process.

It should be pointed out that the pupils too play a part in this matter: Swedish informants state that quite a few handicapped pupils themselves want to attend a special school or at least a special class. They are tired of always being the last one, of always needing extra instruction, of always having to play and talk with adults and/or of missing a large part of what is going on in the class (e.g. hard-of-hearing pupils). Particularly during adolescence these children need contact with pupils who have comparable handicaps and thus form a more suitable peer group.

It can be concluded that the 'working unit' model is elaborated in different ways in practice. In working units that function properly, integration is realised at the curricular level for a substantial number of pupils, whereas in other schools the integration of regular and special education bears a more physical and social character.

DISCUSSION

Big changes in an educational system take time. Against this background, a great deal has happened in Sweden since LGR 80 came into force in 1983. Many special schools have been closed and a number of types of special education have been abolished. The pupils who attended them now go to the Grundskola. This development has undeniably enlarged the possibilities for the integration of handicapped pupils to a considerable extent. Although integration is not yet without problems, important measures have been taken to develop integration. Considered from the viewpoint of the Swedish ideology of equality (see p. 41 above), social integration of handicapped pupils is the least that should be attained in the educational system.

More fundamental forms of integration, such as curricular integration, which are particularly aimed at in the 'working unit' model, are not yet realised satisfactorily everywhere. Many teachers and teacher teams tend to pass on pupils with problems – especially children with the more severe problems, such as social and emotional disturbances – to the special education teacher, preferably in a separate class. New policy initiatives have been taken to give the integration process a new impetus.

It is of great importance to the Swedes to make integration a success. That so much progress has been realised in such a short period is undoubtedly related to the fact that the ideological starting points have been accepted throughout society. This does not mean there is no resistance. Opponents think that the integration process has been implemented too rigidly and they point to the negative effect that integration has had, according to them, on the educational level and the fact that a number of pupils with special needs prefer to have their own schools. They also think that the social and curricular integration in the working units is disappointing. The opponents have difficulty in justifying these claims because there has been little research into the effects of the integration of special needs pupils.

In view of the facts that this integration is socially broadly based, and that the government is willing to continue investing in supporting it, a reversal in Swedish educational policy is not to be expected for the time being.

5

UNITED STATES

Sip Jan Pijl

INTRODUCTION

It is difficult to obtain an accurate picture of regular and special education in the United States, not only because the organisation and practice of education differ from state to state, but also because education in the United States changes continually. In the last decades regular and special education have been shaped by the Elementary and Secondary Education Act, the Education for All Handicapped Children Act (EHA, now Individuals with Disabilities Education Act, IDEA) and the Regular Education Initiative (REI). In this period services for handicapped pupils in regular and special education have improved greatly. The basic principle in the EHA is to educate handicapped pupils in the – for them – Least Restrictive Environment, that is, to educate them as far as possible with non-handicapped children in the regular class or school. Despite the adoption of the Least Restrictive Environment as a guiding principle, growing numbers of students receive (part-time) separate special services. Under the REI attempts are made to further integrate regular and special education.

THE EDUCATIONAL SYSTEM

Structure

Elementary education in the United States comprises one or two years' kindergarten and six to eight years' primary education. In general, children enter kindergarten at the age of 5 and the elementary school when they are 6 years. Each state defines the compulsory school age, ordinarily guaranteeing at least nine years of schooling.

The duration of elementary education depends on the organisation of secondary education in a given school district. The six-year elementary school is the most usual form. Secondary education starts with the seventh or ninth grade and takes six or four years, according to the 6–3–3 scheme or the 8–4 scheme. The first variant prevails: six years of primary education are followed by three years' junior high school and three years' senior high school. Other possibilities are 6–6 and 5–3–4.

In primary education the emphasis has always been on 'the three Rs' (reading, writing, arithmetic), plus subjects such as biology, history, geography, music, drawing, handicraft and physical education. Secondary education has a compulsory programme, the common core, consisting of English, science, social studies, mathematics and physical education. Apart from that, a number of optional subjects can be followed such as one or more foreign languages, Latin, arts, music and vocational subjects.

The big high schools usually offer three 'tracks' that prepare the students for higher education: academic or college-bound, vocational and general (Deen, 1983). After high school several possibilities for further education exist: two years' college, technical institute, four years' college or university.

The education participation figures are high. In 1989, more than 90 per cent of the 5-year-olds went to a kindergarten, while 99 per cent of the 6–15-year-olds attended a school. The number of dropouts in education varies considerably from state to state. In urban areas, for instance Philadelphia, this can amount to 10 per cent. In 1989, 42 million pupils (age group 6–17) in the US followed education.

Legislation, administration and policy

The history of the United States is relatively young compared to Europe's. As a consequence of the dynamics of a developing society, education has always had a pragmatic character, thus making it possible for important social movements to leave their marks on education.

Apart from the *circa* 600,000 native Americans, the United States is peopled by immigrants and the descendants of immigrants from Europe, Africa, Asia and Latin America. The unprecedentedly high immigration levels in the twentieth century have had important consequences for education and the way educational aims are looked at. From the start, education has been multicultural, and has always been considered a means to create unity out of a diverse population.

The foundation of the present constitution and the organisation of education were laid on the east coast and from there spread by colonists. This process has strongly determined the features of the current educational system, especially the high degree of decentralisation of educational government and administration.

Within the federal system, the fifty states carry major responsibilities, particularly in the field of education, which has traditionally been an area in which the role of the federal government is modest. For many years (until 1983), there was not even a federal department of education. (In those days education was subsumed within the department of Health, Education and Welfare.) Although each state has its own educational legislation, which has resulted in many differences between the states, the basic elements of the system are alike.

The control of the implementation and observance of the law is in the hands of the State Board of Education. Each state, except for Hawaii, is divided into school districts that have a high degree of autonomy within the federal legislation. The *circa* 16,000 school districts decide on educational taxes, administer school buildings and take care of the construction of new schools, appoint teachers and other staff, determine salaries, decide on educational policy and are responsible for the day-to-day running of education in a district. Districts sometimes co-operate for the purpose of certain matters, such as the enforcement of the law on special education. In these cases a so-called 'intermediate level' arises.

So the American public school is primarily a school of the local community, administered by the local citizenry and mainly financed with local taxes. As a result of the way education is financed, there are enormous differences with regard to facilities between states and districts. This is disadvantageous for children living in economically weak communities, even if they receive the majority of federal support. An international study of national education systems has shown that differences between schools, in terms of performance, are twice as large in the US as they are in West European countries (OECD, 1981b).

Though parents have always been an important factor in education, US education has not developed along denominational lines to the same extent as countries like the Netherlands for example. Besides the public education system, there are some private schools, mostly of a religious character. That parents are critical observers of the pattern of values that is taught their children at school, appears from the existence of, for instance, the Moral Majority, an extreme right-wing movement in political as well as religious matters and the so-called 'Back to Basics' movement. The latter wants education to focus attention on the three Rs (reading, writing and arithmetic). In a sense, this movement goes back to the so-called Sputnik effect. The launching of the Sputnik in Russia (1957) led to criticism directed against educational results. It was claimed that the high schools lacked intellectual rigour, and education was failing to produce expert scientists (Deen, 1983; OECD, 1981b).

This soon led to political action; the federal government and Congress came up with new legislation in 1958 that laid down federal support for secondary and higher education. This law became known as the National Defence Education Act (OECD, 1981b). Moreover, a test mania grew in the schools. This has persisted right up to the present, with large numbers of tests being administered over the entire educational field. Test results are regarded as a valuable means of establishing student progress and adjusting instruction to the needs of students. Critics argue that the continuous flow of test results exaggerates the differences within schools; by creating a clear division within schools in terms of academic achievement, testing becomes an instrument that contributes to the maintenance of social inequality.

Besides the above-mentioned talent hunting, there was a growing concern in the fifties that a large part of the population, the so-called disadvantaged, lived in poor circumstances. This concern, amongst others, was expressed in the Civil Rights Movement. In the early sixties, this and other movements resulted in the 'War against poverty', an extensive legislative programme the main purpose of which was to break the poverty cycle (OECD, 1981b). The President's Task Force on Education under the chairmanship of John W. Gardner, which published a report in 1964, played an important role in the preparation of the legislative framework of compensatory education for the disadvantaged (e.g. Head Start, Upward Bound). The Task Force drew attention to the large inequalities among states and among districts with regard to educational financing and recommended a general federal educational support, based on 'equalisation formulas', although pessimism existed regarding the feasiblity of this proposition. Moreover, the Task Force indicated that American education had been mainly directed at the 'mainstream' up to then, while gifted pupils on the one hand and poor and mentally and/or physically handicapped pupils on the other had been neglected (OECD, 1981b).

In 1965, the ESEA (Elementary and Secondary Education Act) led to a great breakthrough. The effort to achieve equal opportunities in education was no longer focused only on children who were deprived through poverty, race or cultural backgrounds, but also on the mentally and physically handicapped (see also 'Special needs education', below). Within the ESEA programme, the resources were divided over the following target groups:

1   Pre-school children (by means of a programme called 'Head Start').
2   Nursery school children and children from the lower grades of elementary education.
3   Mentally and physically handicapped children.
4   High school students (by means of vocational training).
5   College students (by means of Basic Educational Opportunity Grants (BEOGs) for higher education).

Poverty and school performance are closely related in the US. Special education, therefore, cannot be seen apart from the compensatory programmes and the like that were started in the sixties with so much enthusiasm (there were about 120 in 1978), in the conviction that education would be able to bring about social changes such as relieving poverty and social disadvantage. However, despite all the efforts that have been spent on compensatory programmes, second language education, other forms of multicultural education and the abolition of legal regulations concerning the segregation of black and white, the average academic achievement of students from the minority groups is still disappointing. The belief that it is possible to remove social disadvantages by means of education is contested by, among others, the Coleman Report that appeared in 1966 (OECD, 1981b) and numerous evaluation studies of compensatory programmes (Jencks, 1972). The unfulfilled expectations nevertheless seem to have had little influence on the programmes, while the 'Back to Basics' movement had; there used to be a broad range of educational aims, but now there is more emphasis on the basic skills.

SPECIAL NEEDS EDUCATION

Developments in special education

Special education first appeared in the US at the beginning of the nineteenth century, a period of great optimism and belief in human capacities. The impetus for this came mainly from Europe. Many Americans went there to study and to acquire knowledge about (the education of) handicapped children. After his study in Paris, Thomas Gallaudet founded a school for the hearing impaired in Connecticut in 1817. Samuel Howe went to England to specialise in teaching methods for the visually impaired and in 1831 he became director of the Perkins school for the blind. In 1848 he also started an experimental programme for the education of mentally handicapped pupils. In the same year, Seguin too came to the US, where he occupied himself for years with the founding of institutions for the mentally handicapped and with the development of programmes for this group (Juul, 1987).

The belief in the educability of mentally handicapped people, however, was diminishing more and more, partly also influenced by social Darwinism, a philosophy that was supported by racist theories from psychologists, sociologists and doctors. This led to the so-called 'eugenic alarm', leading to a neglect of handicapped people and their isolation from society (Juul, 1987).

This only came to an end after the Second World War, not as a consequence of scientific progress, but as the result of a growing moral indignation voiced by a better-informed public. Juul (1987) mentions several factors that played a role in this change of public opinion:

— private initiatives of civilians and civil organisations with regard to the treatment of children with special needs;
— foreign influences, like the educational explorations of (President) Kennedy in the Netherlands, Scandinavia and Russia in the early sixties, the adaptation of the Scandinavian normalisa-

tion principle and the impetus that was given by many leading figures from the field of the humanities who had left Europe because of the war and had settled in the US (Bruno Bettelheim, Kurt Lewin, Marianne Frostig and many others);
— professional organisations, like the Council for Exceptional Children (CEC), founded in 1922 for the well-being of children with special needs in education.

Organisations like the CEC and also parents' organisations have acted as advocacy groups; they have exerted pressure on the authorities by means of, among other things, lawsuits, in order to improve the educational situation. From 1953 on, there were a great many court cases that resulted in, for example, a revision of assessment procedures and the statutory obligation for regular schools to admit handicapped children (ibid.).

In general, the federal contribution to special education policy and financing was rather detached. In 1966 special education was set up as a special division within the Department of Health, Education and Welfare and a start was made with the financing of programmes in the field of special education. In the years following, the role of the federal government in this area increased, also as a result of the above-mentioned judicial decisions that allowed the handicapped the right to education under the equality and protection clause of the national constitution (Juul, 1987).

The increasing federal involvement in special education resulted in the introduction of Public Law 94–142, The Education for All Handicapped Children Act. The period preceding its introduction became known as 'the quiet revolution'. This refers to a process that started in 1970. Over the entire US, the identification, classification, evaluation and assessment procedures concerning handicapped children were criticised and became the subject of lawsuits and legal actions. It turned out that pupils were often misclassified, resulting in wrong placements. On the one hand, this was ascribed to inadequate evaluation instruments and procedures. Intelligence tests, for example, were often culturally biased (based on white standards), the consequence of which was that children from minority groups were often misclassified. On the other hand, incorrect decision-making procedures were established. Traditionally, such decisions were taken unilaterally, on the basis of data of a limited or inappropriate kind, without a legal basis and with a minimum of parental involvement (Abeson and Zettel, 1981).

There was also strong evidence to indicate that referral and placement were a function of administrative convenience rather than being based on the child's individual needs.

The quiet revolution reached its climax in April 1975. In more than half of the states there had been lawsuits in the aforementioned fields. Nevertheless it appeared that even in 1975 more than 1.75 million handicapped children were still excluded from education, solely because of their handicaps, and that more than half of the handicapped children did not receive an appropriate education or had been placed in the wrong educational setting. The necessity of more stringent regulations was obvious and all of this finally resulted in an entirely new federal legislation, which brought about a radical change in the education and care of handicapped children: Public Law 94–142, The Education for All Handicapped Children Act. Signed in November 1975 by President Ford, this Act came partly into effect in September 1978 and became fully operative in 1980.

The general aim of this Act is described as follows: 'It is the purpose of this Act to assure that all handicapped children have available to them, within the time periods specified, free appropriate public education which emphasises special education and related services designed to meet their unique needs' (Abeson and Zettel, 1981, p. 368). The Act defines handicapped children as: children who are mentally retarded, hard-of-hearing, deaf, physically handicapped, health impaired, speech impaired, visually handicapped or seriously emotionally disturbed or who have specific learning problems to such an extent that they need special education and further support (Bateman and Herr, 1981). Special education is described as: 'specially designed instruction, at no cost to parents or guardians, to meet the unique needs of a handicapped child, including classroom instruction, instruction in physical education, home instruction and instruction in hospital and institutions' (Abeson and Zettel, 1981, p. 371). In general, the Act comprises the following aspects (Abeson and Zettel, 1981; Juul, 1987; Wolfendale, 1982):

a   All handicapped children between 3 and 21 years of age are entitled to free education. In principle, the child should be

allowed to participate in/make a choice from all the programmes and activities offered by the school.
b Special education should take place in 'the least restrictive
environment':

> each state must establish procedures to ensure that, to the
> maximum extent appropriate, handicapped children, in-
> cluding children in public and private institutions or
> other care facilities, are educated with children who are
> not handicapped and that special classes, separate school-
> ing, or the removal of handicapped children from the
> regular education environment occurs only when the na-
> ture or severity of the handicap is such that education in
> regular classes with the use of supplementary aids and
> services cannot be achieved satisfactorily.
>
> (Abeson and Zettel, 1981, pp. 372–3; Public
> Law 94–142, 1975, sec. 612, 5, B).

c A central issue of the Act is the IEP (Individualized Education
Program); such a plan has to be made for every handicapped
child and should be put down in writing. The following matters
should be included:
1 present level of educational performance;
2 long-term educational aims (for one year) and short-
term educational aims;
3 specific educational facilities needed to enable the child
to participate in regular education programmes;
4 information concerning the start and duration of these
facilities, and the criteria and evaluation procedures by
which it can be assessed to what extent the aims have
been attained, minimally at year-level.

The IEP is drawn up by an officer of the local education agency
(LEA) in close collaboration with the teacher(s). Both parents
and, if necessary, the child itself have to be involved in drawing
up the plan.
d Parents have the right to see all the documents that concern
their child and to demand a hearing in case of disagreement on
a (decision on) placement.
e Tests and evaluation materials should not be culturally biased
and have to be formulated and/or administered in the child's
mother tongue or in its own way of communication.

f   The federal government is obliged to contribute to the costs for special education.

Singer and Butler (1987) have taken stock of the changes brought about by PL 94–142 in special education. They state that the Act has been an effective instrument of social reform, through its direct influence on local special education programmes. After the Act was introduced, states and districts had to meet quite a number of requirements in order to be eligible for federal money: identification of pupils, individual diagnostics, drawing up written IEPs, placement in the least restrictive environment, informing parents and providing educational support facilities. In addition, all this had to be done with few extra financial resources and a lot of participants with sometimes diverging interests.

How did the process of change take place and what changes occurred? Anticipating PL 94–142, most states had already started to adjust their special education legislation in *circa* 1975. About five years later, each of the districts studied by Singer and Butler (1987) turned out to have adequately integrated the required facilities for special education into their educational programmes. One of the first things the districts took up was the IEP, because this fitted reasonably well with the earlier practice of the local education agencies.

Changes in the number and size of supporting services took place later than the above-mentioned procedural reforms. These changes were generally difficult to implement, more expensive and less easy to control. This concerned, among other things, changes in placement options, class size, training and supporting services. Contrary to what one might expect, PL 94–142 did not lead to radical changes in placement procedures. 'Mainstreaming', the integration of children with special needs into regular classes, was not a new concept for most large LEAs around 1977. At that time, already over 90 per cent of all special education pupils attended regular schools and two-thirds received much of their education in regular classes.

As far as the changes in placement procedures are concerned, two movements can be distinguished:

1   the severely handicapped: from state institutions to public school facilities and from separate to regular schools;
2   the less severely handicapped: more pupils to resource rooms,

more non-categorical placements and fewer self-contained classrooms.

For some districts, the mainstreaming ideology simply was the cheapest solution. This meant that the decision to place a less severely handicapped child in a regular class was often based on economic grounds and not always for the benefit of the child (Singer and Butler, 1987).

The special education population

Since the introduction of the Act, the number of pupils receiving some form of special education has been growing steadily in a declining population. The percentage of 6–17-year-olds was 6.7 in 1977 and has grown to 9.5 per cent in 1989 (Department of Education, 1990).

Across states this figure ranges from 6.2 per cent (Hawaii) to 14.8 per cent (Massachusetts). It may be that state-to-state variation in the percentage of students served is related to state classification procedures, resulting in larger or smaller numbers of students. Other causes of state-to-state variation may include: data reporting practices, state funding formulas and differences in student populations.

An important part of the growth may be attributed to increases in the number of students served as learning disabled, emotionally disturbed and multihandicapped. For instance, in the last decade the number of learning disabled students (LD) has more than doubled (from 0.8 million to 1.9 million). It should be noted that the number of students served as mentally retarded and speech impaired (the latter, however, growing during the last few years) has fallen since 1977. The other handicapping conditions account for no more than 3.6 per cent of all students served and are fairly stable in number.

Another growth factor can be found among children aged 3–5 years. Especially after the 1986 Education of the Handicapped Act amendments, which provided substantial incentives for expanding services to this population, the pace of growth quickened dramatically.

Referral and placement

According to PL 94–142 a decision-making process concerning whether or not a child is eligible for special education is only started when a pupil is put forward for referral, which in many cases is done by the regular class teacher. The decision making is based on a multi-disciplinary case-study evaluation (Pugach, 1985). After the child has been referred, he or she is generally examined by one or more experts, among whom is usually a school psychologist. Next, the diagnostic information is discussed in a special education team meeting in which it is decided how the pupil should be classified and if they should proceed to placement of the child in a form of special education.

There are large differences between states, but also within states with regard to the types of pupils who are regarded as handicapped and receive special education on the basis of this classification. A study by Chalfant in 1980 (Ysseldyke, 1987) has shown that different terms are used in state guidelines for the description of the LD population and that differences exist from state to state in the type and the number of criteria by which it is determined whether a pupil should be classified as 'learning disabled'.

Moreover, according to Voelker Morsink *et al.* (1987) the definitions of LD, ED (emotionally disturbed) and EMR (educable mentally retarded) are not only inconsistent over states (the percentage of children classified as LD varied in 1989 from 2.1 per cent in Georgia to 7.7 per cent in Rhode Island, the percentage ED from 0.04 in Mississippi to 2.2 in Utah and the percentage EMR from 0.4 in New Jersey to 3.3 in Alabama), but also inconsistent in time: several states have repeatedly revised their definitions since the introduction of PL 94–142. Algozzine, Morsink and Algozzine (1988) conclude that there is very little consensus, either conceptually or in practice, on the definition of learning difficulties or the criteria for classifying children as learning disabled.

If a child is to be placed in special education, an officer of the local education agency draws up an Individualized Education Program (IEP) in close co-operation with the teacher and the parents. The rights of the parents in this matter are extensively described by the law. Through the principles of non-discriminatory assessment, multiple evaluation measures and team-based decision making, current federal special education policy attempts to prevent pupils from being inaccurately classified (Pugach, 1985). The effects of this policy at the local level, however, are often not in accordance with the original intentions. Despite the federal regulations, it turns out in practice that the decision of a teacher to refer a pupil for special education is crucial in the entire identification process and that it controls this process to an important degree (Shinn, Tindal and Spira, 1987). Weatherley and Lipsky (1981) use the term 'street level bureaucracy' to indicate how policy is in fact determined by experts in the front line (such as teachers). The original description given of a pupil by the teacher has a major influence on the opinions, judgements and descriptions that are subsequently made by diagnosticians. Besides, it appears that the original, primary impressions have a tendency to persist, even if new light is thrown upon them by fresh data (Pugach, 1985).

Each year 3–5 per cent of the total school population is referred for psychological educational assessment; 92 per cent of these are tested and 73 per cent are referred to special education and are often placed in resource rooms for the mildly handicapped (Pugach, 1985; Ysseldyke, 1987). So in practice it turns out that once a pupil has been identified by the teacher as eligible for special education, and referred as such, it is very likely that the pupil will end up in a form of special education. Moreover, it appears that special education placement often implies 'dead-end-placement'; it is unusual for pupils to return to regular education programmes (Ysseldyke, 1987).

On the basis of extensive research Ysseldyke (1987) concludes that the decision-making processes of special education teams are weak. The only thing a team usually does is to verify problems that have already been observed by the teacher. Despite the fact that many data are reported at the meeting, decision making is often not based on this information. Moreover, frequent use is made of technically inadequate tests. When confronted with this information, diagnostic personnel often replied that they mainly rely on their 'clinical judgment' (Ysseldyke, 1987).

Decisions appear to be especially related to the extent to which a teacher wants to have a pupil in the class and to pupil characteristics such as sex, socio-economic status, physical appearance and ethnic background (Gerber and Semmel, 1984).

The placement options for handicapped children are:

1   Regular class: students receive the majority of their education in the regular class and receive special education for less than 21 per cent of the school day in or outside the regular class.
2   Resource room: students receive special education for 21–60 per cent of the school day and participate in the regular class for the remaining part of the day.
3   Separate class: students receive special education for more than 60 per cent of the school day with part-time instruction in the regular class.
4   Separate school facility: students receive special education in separate day schools (or residental facilities) for more than 50 per cent of the school day.

Within these placement options special services can have a variety of forms: itinerant services (individual instruction in a small group from supporting personnel such as a speech therapist), in-class services (additional help in the regular class from tutors, aides, interpreters) or services to the teacher (the child's teacher receives additional support).

The vast majority of students with special needs receive services in regular school buildings, that is in regular classes (29 per cent), resource rooms (40 per cent) or separate classes (24 per cent) (these percentages apply for 6–21-year-olds) (Department of Education, 1990). Only 5 per cent of the children with special needs are educated in a separate school.

The placement options that are available for the different groups of students with special needs are shown in Table 5.1.

INTEGRATION

The connection between regular and special education

In many respects the US is a country of large numbers. This certainly holds for the size of most schools in the US. Because of the large pupil population within elementary schools it is possible to work with two to three parallel classes per grade. Many schools make these parallel groups as homogeneous as possible by separating slow and fast learners. As a result, teachers in the US have been accustomed to working in fairly homogeneous classes as far as level is concerned (Jenkins, personal communication, 1989; Zig-

Table 5.1 United States: percentage of children and youth, age 6–21, served in different educational environments, by handicapping condition: school year 1987–8

Handicapping condition	Reg. class	Res. room	Sep. class	Sep. school	Resid. facility	Home/ hospital
Learning disabled	17.6	59.2	21.7	1.4	0.1	0.1
Speech impaired	74.8	19.7	3.8	1.5	0.1	0.1
Mentally retarded	5.7	24.0	57.6	11.4	1.0	0.3
Emotionally disturbed	12.6	32.9	34.6	14.3	3.5	2.2
Hard of hearing and deaf	24.4	20.9	35.2	10.8	8.6	0.2
Multihandicapped	6.4	13.3	45.9	27.2	4.0	3.1
Orthopaedically impaired	27.8	18.0	31.8	13.2	1.0	8.3
Other health impaired	30.6	20.8	18.7	9.5	0.8	19.6
Visually handicapped	37.7	25.6	20.8	5.4	10.0	0.6
Deaf-blind	8.9	7.2	35.1	21.0	24.2	3.7
All conditions	28.9	40.0	24.7	4.9	0.8	0.7

Source: Department of Education, 1990
Notes: Totals include data from the fifty states, District of Columbia and Puerto Rico.
Educational placements for children age 3–5 are not reported by handicapping condition.

mond, personal communication, 1989). In such classes a standard programme for all pupils can be followed and the pressure for differentiation within a class is not very high. In this context regular teachers tend to regard deviant pupils as a problem. For these pupils the standard programme is inappropriate, and adjusting the programme within the normal class structure is considered highly problematic. For pupils who are unable or unwilling to follow the regular programme special measures have been taken. Besides the aforementioned special education (with different programmes, for example for the hearing impaired, learning disabled, socially and emotionally disturbed, physically handicapped) there are also extensive programmes for the so-called Chapter I-pupils (pupils who score in the lower percentiles of school achievement test scores), for gifted pupils, for migrant children, for bilingual children and so on. So as soon as children deviate from the average, attempts are made to make provision for them by means of a separate programme. In the words of Will (1986, p. 1), the purpose is quite explicitly: 'to bring them into contact with a more effective teacher and program'. The programmes for pupils who deviate in any respect are mostly of the so-called pull-out type: for part of the time, the pupils concerned leave the regular class and attend, for instance, the resource room. For Chapter I-pupils, however, this is not always the case; some Chapter I-teachers come into the classes to work separately with the Chapter I-children.

The implication of the foregoing is that regular teachers are still responsible for deviating pupils for substantial amounts of time. A great deal of the teaching in the subjects that present difficulties is provided by others or elsewhere, but for the rest pupils with problems follow the standard regular programme. In practice, however, it turns out that the regular teacher does not adjust the programme to these pupils and does not know what the special teacher does in pull-out time (for example, the regular teacher has no copy of the IEP). It appears that in the American system the pupil is split up into a part that has no problem and a part that is problematic. For the latter someone else (other than the class teacher) is responsible, so differentiation in the classroom is considered unnecessary. If, for example in the case of behavioural problems, this position cannot be maintained, the pupil is referred to a full-time self-contained classroom.

Although American education under PL 94–142 is generally seen as integrated, there is little curricular integration in the practice outlined above. Pupils with educational needs that deviate from the average are taken out of the classroom and are supported by special teachers. In the regular programme little or nothing changes. For pupils in the self-contained classroom social integration is also hampered.

A crucial problem in all this seems to be that regular and special teachers have limited contact with each other. Since their training and experience are very different, they also have different interpretations of their tasks in practice. The regular teacher teaches large groups of pupils and thinks that the special teacher is not capable of this through lack of experience in regular classes. The special teacher is seen as someone who works with small groups of pupils in a way that is sometimes removed from daily school practice. The special teacher, on the other hand, regards the regular teacher as someone who is not capable of doing more than carrying out standard programmes and who has no response when confronted with slightly deviating educational needs (Zigmond, personal communication, 1989).

Against this background it is not surprising that the two groups only co-operate with difficulty. There is in fact little or no contact between them. The regular teacher will not readily ask advice from the special teacher for a pupil who is at risk. And if this does happen in an informal context, the advice will be in most cases to ask for a test, because it is far more advantageous to the special education teacher to guide the pupil for part of the time through a referral than counselling the regular teacher without any compensation of time.

In summary, given the differences in training and role perceptions in addition to the resourcing constraints, it is understandable that the two groups have limited collaboration. As a consequence, the integration of regular and special education is limited.

Will's position paper

The growing awareness that the goals concerning the integration of pupils with special needs, as laid down in PL 94–142, have not been realised in all respects has led to a revival of discussion on the position of special education. Will's position paper, published in 1986, was a turning-point in these discussions.

In this paper a clear position is taken. It draws attention to the diffuse nature of the educational offerings presented to pupils with learning problems, partly the result of the large variety in rules and regulations. To illustrate this, Will cites four problem areas:

1 For special pupils special programmes exist. The mere existence of these programmes and the extra money that is involved elicit referrals. The sometimes sharp distinction between programmes leads to all kinds of problems, such as pupils who fall between two programmes or are misclassified.
2 The system of regular and special education is dual: both are administered and financed through separate channels.

Although the two systems coincide at the level of school buildings, the duality impedes co-operation.

3 Pupils can only be offered special education if they are categorised in the required manner. The label and the separation from their classmates, wholly or not, have a stigmatising effect. This can work out negatively for the pupil as well as for the pupil's environment.

4 Parents play an important role in the decisions on referral to special education. In practice, a referral to a special programme quite often leads to conflicts. Schools talk of 'pushy' parents. The co-operation between parents and school, which is so essential, has then been disrupted from the start.

So the most common approach used with pupils with learning problems, the pull-out approach, causes difficulties in practice and has proved to be rather ineffective. In Will's position paper an approach is advocated in which regular education is adapted to pupils with special needs. The problems that are inherent in labelling would then disappear.

A problem in the integration of pupils with learning problems into regular education – and parents especially point this out – is that the problems did develop in regular education, and regular education has not built up expertise in educating these pupils because it tends to pass them on to others (Keogh, 1988). Teachers in regular education also have doubts about the need for and feasibility of educating students with special needs within the regular class (Coates, 1989; Semmel et al., 1991).

Consequently, for a successful integration of regular and special education it is necessary that the expertise of special programmes is transferred to the regular class: 'blending of intrinsic strength of both systems' (Will, 1986, p. 10). It is recognised that several problems have to be solved for this to happen. In regular education, for example, more time will have to be offered for instruction, support will have to be available for the teacher within the building, school boards should be given the responsibility to decide on the expenditure of all funds that have been programme-specific previously, and new teaching methods adjusted to regular education must be developed (Reynolds, Wang and Walberg, 1987).

In Will's position paper the education community was invited to react to the policy outlined in it and submit proposals for integration projects. And so it happened. In several places in the US, experiments with the integration of special and regular education were set up. Within this framework also training programmes for regular teachers were developed, research was set up and pupils with a statutory entitlement to a special programme were placed with regular pupils in one class.

Will's position paper freed the way for experimenting in practice – sometimes far beyond the existing regulations – with new forms of support for pupils with problems. This led to the designation, the 'Regular Education Initiative' (REI) (Hallahan *et al.*, 1988).

Integration projects

As a consequence of the REI, projects have started in various places in the US. Virtually all of these are aimed at integrating at least parts of special education into regular education. Some projects are focused more on changing regular education in such a way that the outflow to special education will diminish in the long run. Without attempting to offer an exhaustive coverage, we will briefly describe a number of them.

In the so-called MELD (Mainstream Experiences for the Learning Disabled) project the two existing self-contained classrooms of the project school were closed down and the pupils spread among the regular classes. Two children who were considered too difficult beforehand were transferred to other schools. The two special education teachers and their assistants were given other tasks within the school: the assistants work individually or in small groups with the special needs children in the classroom and the special education teachers work as consultants for the regular teachers about 75 per cent of the time, are responsible for materials and work with the pupils in the class. The extra training of teachers has been particularly directed at managing behavioural problems and at aspects of subject matter. Many of the problems that have to be solved daily are behavioural problems. New referrals have hardly occurred within the course of this project. The routine of the regular teachers, however, has not really changed. Their instruction is still mainly teacher-centred and in a number of cases the integrated pupils are still regarded as the responsibility of the special education team (Baker and Zigmond, 1990; Zigmond and Baker, 1990).

The so-called TEAMS project (Tailoring Educational Alternatives for Middle Schools) is characterised by a more gradual integration. The first phase of the project is aimed at strengthening the position in education of pupils with learning problems. It concerns pupils who spend part of the school time in the resource room. Both the regular and the special education teachers are involved. The idea behind this is that, if these pupils are going to perform better and especially if the regular teachers become accustomed to helping them, a more gradual integration of these pupils into regular education will be possible. Pupils from the self-contained classrooms, who are now hardly involved in the project, can be slowly integrated and the number of referrals will drop. The support of the school team at the level of subject matter consists of introducing curriculum-based measurement as a monitoring technique, co-operative learning as a method of working in the classroom and support in reading instruction.

The ISSAQUAH school district project has drawn a lot of attention with its 'Integrated Classroom Model' (ICM). In the ICM an integrated class is built up for two-thirds of pupils with minimally average level and for one-third of pupils with learning problems (this concerns LD, EMR, emotionally disturbed, visually impaired, hearing impaired and orthopaedically impaired children). The underlying philosophy is that the teacher does not have to spend too much time on the 'moderate' pupils and thus is free to support pupils with learning problems. Moreover, the 'good' pupils can serve as models for the other children and take over part of the teacher's task in the instruction of the pupils with problems (co-operative learning is a key word here as well). In the age groups from 10 to 11 years on, the difference in level between the two groups becomes rather large, however, which causes problems in practice.

The other regular pupils (below average) are in regular classes (note that schools are big enough to have two or more parallel classes at each level). Each ICM class receives additional support for three hours by means of an education assistant (an assistant with only on-the-job training). The Integrated Classroom Model started in 1980. ICM teachers are certified in special education as well as in regular education. During the project the percentage of referrals has not decreased; on the contrary, it has grown. This is ascribed to an enlarged diagnostic insight on the part of teachers.

74

An alternative explanation would be that regular classes (non-ICM), populated by below-average pupils, not provided with any form of extra support and surrounded by well-supported ICM classes, can only benefit from quick referrals. For this is in the interests of the pupil and the regular class as well as the funding of the entire system. ICM classes are highly performance-oriented units. Children with behavioural problems, severely learning disabled children, children with Down's syndrome and so on are referred to other schools with self-contained classrooms.

The evaluation of the project shows that there are some differences between ICM schools and non-ICM schools. Social integration does seem to improve a little, but academic performance effects have not been observed. Pupils with learning problems in the ICM classes, however, seem to perform better in the high school period. Parents of children with learning problems are very satisfied with ICM (Affleck *et al.*, 1988; Madge, Affleck and Lowenbraun, 1990).

A more advanced form of integration is aimed at by the MERGE project (Maximizing Educational Remediation within General Education). The project started in 1981/2. Initially it was based on a 'teacher consultation' model, directed at the development of problem-solving behaviour and interventions in the classroom in order to prevent referrals (Wood and MacDonald, 1988). At first, the school psychologist acted as a consultant. Later, this task was taken over by a TAT (Teacher Assistance Team) consisting of a few regular teachers chosen by their colleagues. After a year a TAT can be partly replaced. The TAT members are assigned time for class observations and consultation. They can also draw on more specialised expertise in and near the school. More recently, the TAT method has been supplemented with in-service training for the regular teachers and, at the teachers' request, a behavioural problems specialist has been taken on.

The pupils are categorised according to age into so-called home classes. In the home class they are divided into ability groups for reading, arithmetic, etc. In principle, each level group is assigned to a classroom (a home class may contain as many as eighty pupils). Each group within the home class has its own teacher plus special education assistants or volunteers for a number of hours. The support of teachers and the school organisation set up in the project have resulted in a decrease in the number of referrals by 80 per cent. The TAT model clearly works as a pre-referral strategy. Successes as in the MERGE project have also been reported elsewhere (see Reynolds, 1990). Pupils with learning/behavioural problems remain in the regular classes (often the lowest level group). Generally, schools still have a self-contained class for the most severely handicapped. It should be noted that pupils from this group participate in regular classes up to 50 per cent of the school time. Extra help is provided then. The strong decline in the number of referrals has led to problems in the financing of the project. Therefore, the school population is now screened yearly by means of a number of standardised tests so that the required percentage of special education pupils is at least officially present. For this group the statutory IEP is drawn up.

One of the best-known and most visible ongoing programmes to integrate handicapped students in regular education is the Adaptive Learning Environments Model (ALEM). The basic idea in ALEM is that all students learn in different ways and require varying amounts of instruction and time to learn, and that instructional programmes should be adapted to their particular needs. Instructional offerings to meet the needs of individual students are made available in the regular classroom setting to all students, both those with special needs and their 'regular' classroom peers. The thrust of ALEM is to move away from placement decisions towards decisions on (individual) instructional programmes.

In the elaboration of this idea ALEM integrates aspects of individualised prescriptive education (basic skills mastery) with aspects of informal education that foster self-responsibility (Wang, Peverly and Randolph, 1984). The implementation of ALEM is supported by an ongoing, databased, staff development approach, instructional teaming, multi-age grouping and a parent involvement programme.

Several publications make claims for the feasibility and effectiveness of ALEM as a full-time mainstreaming programme for moderately handicapped students. The overall conclusion is that under ALEM instructional provisions can be adapted effectively to the needs of most students, such as EMR, LD and SED (severely emotionally disturbed) classifications (Wang et al., 1984; Wang and Birch, 1984a, 1984b; Wang, Gennari and Waxman, 1985). A review by Fuchs and Fuchs (1988) casts another light on ALEM: 'there is insufficient cause to view it as a successful, large-scale, full-time mainstreaming programme' (p. 126).

DISCUSSION

In the US a revival of the integration between regular and special education is going on: the 'Regular Education Initiative' (Hallahan *et al.*, 1988). The basis for the REI is in fact nothing more than dissatisfaction with the integration practice under PL 94–142. The maintenance of special programmes is expensive and diagnostic decisions on placements in programmes are contestable (Ysseldyke and Algozzine, 1982). Further, there are serious doubts about the effectiveness of pull-out programmes (Epps and Tindall, 1987; Leinhardt, Bickel and Pallay, 1982) and there is only rarely talk of real integration. At the same time, however, there is little scientific support for the assumption that the regular class is the most appropriate place for a wide range of pupils, including those with problems (see, among others, Carnine and Kameenui, 1990; Hallahan *et al.*, 1988; Kauffman, Gerber and Semmel, 1988). It is also not known precisely what changes should be made in regular education in order to provide adequate education for all pupils. The REI provoked high levels of confusion, emotion and debate. For some the REI is a code word for full inclusion or the elimination of special education. For others it is an effort to persuade and assist classroom teachers in accepting a greater responsibility for instructing students with disabilities (Jenkins and Pious, 1991).

In other words, in the REI the will to integrate comes first and the consequences for education and for pupils remain to be developed later. Jenkins (personal communication, 1989) puts it this way: 'The REI focuses on integration, not on education.'

Now that the implementation of REI ideas is in full blast, the first results of evaluation studies are becoming available. In these studies the two above-mentioned issues are central: the method of implementation and the effects on pupils.

As regards the implementation method, the regular teacher is central in the REI: the regular teacher is the one who is ultimately responsible for the education of the pupils (Jenkins, Pious and Jewell, 1990). This is also what the projects have in common. For the rest, there is such an enormous diversity in the establishment and rationale of the projects that one gets the impression that the starting point does not really matter. Whether it is the gradual approach of TEAMS, the rigour of MELD (though far more rigorous ones called 'Rights without labels' exist), the somewhat overorganised approach of ISSAQUAH or the mainly teacher-oriented ALEM and MERGE, they all realise forms of integration between special and regular education. There are also large differences with regard to the preparation and support of teachers. It almost seems that it is not so much the kind of training and support that is important for teaching in integrated settings, but rather the fact that something is done about training and support. Perhaps the mere fact that they are working on increasing their professionalism gives teachers the feeling that they are able to cope with their task in integrated settings (compare with the teacher efficacy studies; Meijer, 1988).

Evaluation research – as an attempt to map the effects of integration – has been focused on achievement and social integration. Although much evaluation research is still going on, results so far are neutral: integration does not really make a difference as far as achievement or social integration of pupils with special needs is concerned. Calculations with regard to the costs of integrated versus pull-out settings show that there is no financial gain in integration. Partly based on these findings – which are disappointing to advocates of the REI – discussion about the assumptions behind and the objectives for the REI has started again. Opponents of the REI state that the REI addresses the wrong issues in the education of special needs students. They claim that the real issue with the education of students with special needs is not where they will be best served and who will serve them but how to serve them best (Carnine and Kameenui, 1990; Kauffman, 1989). Despite all the obstacles in the integration of regular and special education in the US, it is undeniable that in a large number of integration projects knowledge is developed that may be of importance to mainstreaming and integration policies within and outside the US.

6

ENGLAND AND WALES

Seamus Hegarty

INTRODUCTION

The United Kingdom has separate educational systems for England and Wales, Northern Ireland and Scotland. This discussion is confined to England and Wales. An important feature of the educational system of England and Wales is that the responsibility for education is decentralised. As far as education is concerned, the countries are split up into so-called local education authorities (LEAs) that carry a large part of the responsibility for organising education at local level.

For a long time, England and Wales had separate systems for regular and special education. The law made provision for handicapped children to be classified according to categories of handicap. Approximately 2 per cent of all children were classified as handicapped and went to special schools or units in regular schools. Although it was legally possible to integrate handicapped pupils into regular education, this seldom occurred.

In the sixties and seventies there was a growing discontent with the existence of separate systems of regular and special education. The classification of children according to categories of handicap was no longer considered satisfactory, because it ignored individual differences, social backgrounds and developmental stages. Besides, problems arose with the placement of multiply handicapped pupils who did not fit into one category. Once a child had been placed, the dangers of labelling and of stigmatising arose. Also, under the influence of a growing interest in human rights and the situation of minorities, stimulated among other things by foreign experiences (US, Denmark, Sweden), special education

underwent a period of change and reflection. This was characterised by an increasing resistance to segregated education and a
growing preference for integration. The idea behind this was that
handicapped people should be able to grow up in an environment
that was as normal as possible. In 1974 a Committee of Enquiry
under the chairmanship of Warnock (the so-called Warnock
Committee) was set up to review educational provision for
handicapped children in Great Britain. The ensuing report was
extremely influential in shaping thinking about special educational
provision. The Committee also came up with new procedures for
the identification and assessment of special needs and new thinking on the educational facilities required to meet those needs.

Many of the Warnock recommendations were embodied in the
Education Act 1981. This formally adopted 'special educational
needs' as its conceptual basis in place of the discarded categories
of handicap. The Act built on the recommendations for identifying
and assessing pupils with special needs and placed a new emphasis
on making appropriate provision for them in regular schools.

THE EDUCATIONAL SYSTEM

Structure

Schooling is compulsory between the ages of 5 and 16 years. Public
education is free in all state and assisted (mostly church) schools.
About 7 per cent of pupils attend private fee-paying schools.

Pre-school education is not a statutory requirement and the
availability of provision varies widely. Just under one half of those
aged 3 to 4 years attend nursery school or a nursery class in a
primary school, many of them on a part-time basis. Other options
for children under 5 include various forms of day care provision
and playgroups run on a voluntary basis.

Primary education covers children aged 5 to 11 years. (Some
areas have operated a three-tier system – lower, middle and upper
schools – since the sixties, with transition ages of 8, 9 or 10 and 12
or 13 years respectively.) Most secondary schools (86 per cent) are
comprehensive and seek to cater for pupils with a wide range of
ability. There are some grammar and secondary modern schools
and a few technical schools. A small number of a new kind of school

known as City Technology Colleges have been set up in recent years.

In January 1990, there were 20,891 primary schools and 570 middle schools classified as primary schools in England and Wales; there were 3,311 comprehensive schools, 150 grammar schools, 205 secondary modern schools and four technical schools (Hayes and Le Metais, 1991).

National examinations are taken by the majority of pupils at the age of 16. The most common of these is the General Certificate of Secondary Education (GCSE), which replaced both the General Certificate of Education Ordinary Level (O-level) and the Certificate of Secondary Education (CSE) in 1988. The GCSE consists of a range of examinations in single subjects. The grade awarded is usually based partly on course work done throughout a period of up to two years and partly on a final examination.

Legislation, administration and policy

The Education Act 1944 and subsequent amendments provide the basis for the management of all schools. Major changes were effected by the Education Reform Act 1988. Those most significant for compulsory education are the introduction of a national curriculum and a standard national form of assessment, and the delegation of many financial and management responsibilities from local education authorities to the governing bodies of individual schools. Many of the provisions are set for implementation over a lengthy period of time.

The Secretary of State for Education is responsible for education policy in England, for monitoring the quality of schooling, for deciding the annual grant to local education authorities and for ensuring the effective use of resources. The Secretary of State is assisted in these responsibilities by three junior ministers, a department of state (the Department for Education) and Her Majesty's Inspectorate. Various statutory and other educational organisations are fully or partly funded by the Department for Education, including the National Curriculum Council and the School Examinations and Assessment Council.

Education in Wales (other than university education) is the responsibility of the Secretary of State for Wales. The English and Welsh education systems are identical except that special provision may be made for teaching through the medium of Welsh and there are requirements for the teaching of the Welsh language and other Welsh elements in some subjects within the national curriculum.

Local education authorities are responsible for organising public education services at local level. There are 116 local education authorities in England and Wales. These authorities are run by elected members and are required by law to have an education committee.

The education budget is used for teachers' salaries, the recurrent and maintenance costs of schools, equipment and materials, and central administrative costs, which include the provision of services such as:

— inspectors/advisers
— teachers' centres
— advisory and support units
— a special needs service
— educational psychology service
— educational welfare officers
— careers service
— school library service.

The primary duty of local education authorities is to ensure that there are sufficient schools and teachers to provide efficient education to meet the needs of the population of their area. The role of the local education authority is changing, however, and is likely to face further change in the near future. Strategic responsibilities are becoming more important, with school governing bodies taking on more management functions. Two developments in particular have contributed to these changes: local management of schools, and the introduction of grant-maintained schools.

The introduction of local management of schools, which is being phased in over a period of five years between 1989 and 1994, has radically altered the resourcing context of schools. All secondary schools and many primary schools now have responsibility for their own budgets. Each local education authority is obliged to allocate its overall education budget to schools by means of a formula based essentially on pupil numbers, with some allowance being made for factors such as special educational need and social deprivation. This is having the effect of transferring many financial decisions from local authorities to schools and is likely to have major implications for the central services which local authorities are able to provide.

Grant-maintained schools are a new category of school created as a result of the 1988 Education Act. Schools may if they wish opt out of local authority control and receive their funding directly from the Department for Education. By March 1992 just under 1 per cent of schools nationally had elected to opt out. Where a substantial number of schools in a single authority have opted for grant-maintained status, the local authority's sphere of strategic action is considerably reduced.

All state schools are run by a school governing body which represents the local education authority, the community, the parents and the teaching staff of the school. The governing body must decide the general direction of the school and its curriculum, within the framework laid down by the national curriculum.

The national curriculum, introduced through the 1988 Education Act, consists of the three 'core' subjects of English, mathematics and science plus seven other 'foundation' subjects. For each subject 'attainment targets', specified at up to ten levels of attainment, set out objectives for learning, and 'programmes of study' specify the learning experiences by which the targets may be attained. A complementary system of national assessment is prescribed, with provision for assessing all pupils at the end of each of four key stages. (These occur, respectively, at around the ages of 7, 11, 14 and 16.)

SPECIAL NEEDS EDUCATION

Historical developments and legislation

Just as in other European countries, special education in England and Wales developed over the course of the nineteenth century. Several special schools were founded then, at first for children with sensory impairments, later – when primary education had become widespread – for children with learning problems also. These early special schools were founded mainly as a result of private initiatives and not on the basis of legislation. The emphasis in these schools was directed in the first place at the physical care of the children and only secondarily at education.

In the early part of the twentieth century, local education auth-

83

orities were obliged to make educational provision for certain categories of handicapped pupils. According to the Education Act 1921, handicapped children should only be educated in special schools and classes. This resulted in the development of a separate system of special education, which was in line with the way handicaps were considered at the time: an unchangeable characteristic of a person. There were some attempts to move towards integration in those years. In 1929 the Wood Committee advocated a common educational system for feeble-minded and 'retarded children' (i.e. children who could not keep up at school). This committee held that special and regular education should be brought closer together, legislatively as well as administratively, and that the special school should be regarded as a 'helpful variation' of the regular school.

The next major landmark was the Education Act 1944. This extended the range of children's special needs for which local authorities were obliged to make specific provision. Associated regulations made in 1945 defined eleven categories of handicap (reduced to ten in 1953 by including 'diabetic' within 'delicate'). These provided a framework for provision which lasted for nearly forty years, until the implementation in 1983 of the Education Act 1981.

The 1944 Act was couched in terms of special schools as the prime source of special educational provision, but it did allow that regular schools might play a part in this. Regulations prescribed that blind, deaf, epileptic, physically handicapped and aphasic children were seriously handicapped and had to be educated in special schools. Children with other handicaps might attend regular schools if there were adequate facilities for them.

The limited legislative space to develop integration in this way was, however, barely used, with the notable exception of provision for partially hearing pupils. The regular school system was struggling in the immediate post-war years with inferior accommodation and insufficient trained teachers. Making special educational provision in regular schools was not accorded high priority when resources were strained to provide a basic education for the majority.

For a number of years, then, segregation prevailed. There were in effect two separate systems running in parallel. Special schools catered for the more seriously handicapped pupils, while regular schools provided for the 'non-handicapped'. Regular schools did have their problem pupils and, if they could not off-load them to special schools, provided for them as best they could. This was not always good enough, either because they lacked the expertise or the possibility of giving individual attention or they did not have a commitment to educating these pupils.

The Education (Handicapped Children) Act 1970 was a landmark in the education of those pupils with the greatest difficulties. It mandated that education had to be offered to all children, regardless of the extent or severity of their handicapping conditions. With effect from April 1971 health authorities ceased to provide training for children and young people designated as mentally handicapped, and administrative responsibility for them was transferred to local education authorities. Henceforward, no child is deemed in law to be ineducable, and school places have to be offered to all children.

A Committee of Enquiry was set up in 1974 to review educational provision for handicapped children and young people, and to make recommendations for improving it. The Committee's report (DES, 1978), published in 1978 and widely known as the Warnock Report, was extremely influential and laid the foundations for the Education Act 1981. It adopted the concept of special educational need and reconceptualised the nature of special educational provision. It estimated that about one child in six would require some form of special educational provision, which would be additional to or different from regular educational provision. Among its many recommendations were proposals for abolishing the statutory categories of handicap as the basis for identifying children who required special education, establishing detailed and specific procedures for assessing children with special educational needs and expanding pre-school and post-school provision.

Major changes to the law on special education were introduced in 1981, though not implemented until April 1983. The Education Act 1981 amended key sections of the 1944 Act and became the central law governing special education in England and Wales. It was supplemented in 1983 by a set of regulations that amplified the law on assessments and how they were to be conducted and recorded.

Under the 1981 Act a child has special educational needs if he or she has learning difficulties which are significantly greater than those experienced by the majority of children of the same age or if they have a disability that prevents or hinders them from making use of the educational facilities generally available to age peers. The Act makes a critical distinction within the group characterised in this way. Some children will be the direct responsibility of the local education authority in the sense that they have 'special educational needs which call for the local education authority to determine the special provision that should be made for them'. This implicitly defines two groups of children, those whose education remains the responsibility of the school, and those for whom the local authority must determine provision. The Act has nothing to say on the nature or severity of the needs that would place a child in one or other group, but it can be inferred that the two groups comprise those with lesser and greater needs respectively.

The Act requires that children with special educational needs should be educated in regular schools, subject to account being taken of the wishes of their parents and of three conditions: that the requisite special educational provision can be offered; that the other children in the group can be educated efficiently; and that efficient use is made of resources. The Act also stipulates that if a child with special educational needs is being educated in a regular school, he or she must engage in the activities of the school alongside other children who do not have special educational needs to the greatest extent possible.

As noted above, the Education Reform Act 1988 introduced major changes to state education in England and Wales. Though the Act has little to say about pupils with special educational needs, it is likely to have a major impact on special educational provision. Wedell (1990) and others have commented on the near-total exclusion of pupils with special educational needs from initial drafts. Some improvements were effected subsequently but major anxieties about the consequences for special educational provision persist.

On the positive side, the Act entitles pupils to a broad curriculum. Lewis (1991) proposes four potential benefits for pupils with learning difficulties: a shared curricular framework which makes it more feasible for pupils of different abilities to work alongside each other; a shared curricular language; the guarantee of a broad curriculum that contrasts with many restricted curriculum offerings in the past; and the acknowledged importance of assessing pupils' learning at regular intervals. While much of this reflects existing practice in some special schools, they represent targets still to be achieved in many regular schools.

On the negative side, the implementation of the national curriculum and its associated assessment arrangements could marginalise pupils with special educational needs even more than previously. Hegarty (1993) draws attention to the competitive ideology underpinning the Act. In conjunction with the limited amount of explicit attention paid to pupils with special educational needs, this is argued to 'add greatly to the difficulty of providing education of high quality for pupils with special educational needs'.

The organisation of special education

Special educational provision is defined in the Education Act 1981 as 'educational provision which is additional to, or otherwise different from, the educational provision made generally for children in schools maintained by the local education authority concerned'. About 20 per cent of children are assumed to need special educational provision. For a small proportion – about 2 per cent – this provision is formally determined by the local education authority through an assessment procedure and written down in a Statement of Special Educational Needs. Many though by no means all of these children are educated in special schools. Special educational provision for other pupils takes the form of special classes in regular schools or, more commonly, modifications to mainstream educational provision.

In 1990 there were 1,439 special schools in England and Wales, catering for 1.3 per cent of pupils. About one-quarter were residential. Historically, special schools were grouped by handicapping condition – hearing impairment, physical impairment, educational subnormality and so on, with schools for the educationally subnormal and the physically handicapped being the most numerous. When the official use of categories of handicap was discontinued, information by type of handicap was no longer collected. Individual special schools continued to recruit from their traditional 'constituencies' but schools are beginning to recruit more broadly, with greater reference to pupils' specific educational requirements.

A development to note is the emergence of link schemes between special schools and regular schools. A NFER study examining such schemes in 1985 found that three-quarters of special schools had some timetabled links, in which pupils from the special school spent time working in a regular school (Jowett, Hegarty and Moses, 1988). Many link schemes involved staff as well, both teachers and classroom assistants. Although most staff movement was from the special school to the regular school, there was some in the reverse direction to support specific curriculum development.

There are considerable differences between local education authorities as regards the use of special schools and units. Policies are affected by past practices, budgetary considerations and specific local factors. Some LEAs have pursued a positive policy of integrating into mainstream provision as many children with special needs as possible, and this has resulted in the closure of special schools in some areas. There has been an overall decrease in the use of residential special schools, though this trend has reversed for pupils with emotional and behavioural difficulties.

Voluntary organisations play an important part in special educational provision. Traditionally, they have founded and maintained institutions, especially in the areas of sensory impairment and severe mental handicap, but this has changed as the role of the local education authority has been more clearly defined and there has been more emphasis on placing children within the local community and regular schools. Voluntary organisations still manage some educational institutions but many of these now depend largely on local education authority support; those institutions still surviving are generally highly specialised. Larger agencies, for example Mencap and the Royal National Institute for the Blind, employ professional staff to work in a consultative capacity at both local and national levels.

Special educational provision in regular schools is provided through special classes, either full-time or part-time attendance, or through support given to regular classes. As discussed below, a major focus of contemporary debate is how to insert special educational provision into the 'whole school' so that it becomes an integral part of the school's educational offerings, available to all pupils as need dictates and not just to the traditional clients of special education.

Support services

Special education is supported by a number of services external to the school. These are usually the responsibility of the local education authority, though some are provided by health authorities or social services departments. Some support services are also provided by voluntary sector organisations.

The most important source of support is the learning support service; its principal function is to assist regular schools in the task of educating pupils with learning difficulties. Learning support services vary greatly in structure, mode of working and even title. Some have evolved from peripatetic remedial services; others incorporate the functions of sensory impairment specialists and other staff to form a generic support service to schools.

Staff from learning support services spend much of their time in schools, teaching pupils and advising teachers. The latter is assuming greater importance as regular schools take more responsibility for pupils in the school who have special educational needs. When staff from the learning support service do teach in schools, they are increasingly likely to do so in the classroom as opposed to withdrawing pupils for detached instruction.

Most local education authorities operate specialist peripatetic services for pupils with hearing impairments and those with visual impairments. In addition to teachers, staffing includes sensory impairment specialists and ancillary workers. Staff in these services work in both special schools and regular schools. Functions carried out include assessment, advising teachers, monitoring progress, counselling, in-service training, advising on the use of aids, and working with pre-school children and their parents.

All local education authorities employ advisers/inspectors who are charged with supplying professional advice to the authority and monitoring its educational provision. There has been a considerable increase in the number of special needs advisers in post in recent years. Their main role components include administration, development of provision, teacher support and in-service training.

School psychological services are well-established in most education authorities, and indeed have expanded considerably in recent years. Assessing children and contributing to placement decisions continue as major role activities for psychologists. Traditionally, this has entailed a one-off and relatively static involvement in children's learning difficulties. Many psychologists have reacted against this by seeking closer links with schools and developing quasi-advisory roles.

Referral and placement procedures

The Education Act 1981 and its associated documents set out procedures for identifying children with special educational needs and conducting assessments to establish what their special educational needs actually are. The procedures are of two types, dependent on whether educational provision for the children will remain the responsibility of the school or is determined by the local authority. The distinction relates essentially to the extent and complexity of the individual's special needs: the expectation is that as many children as possible will be dealt with in the school system, without formal involvement of the local authority.

Assessment taking place within the school is intended to be a continuous process, feeding into class teaching and the monitoring of progress. It should be conducted initially by the class teacher and extended progressively, as necessary, to the head teacher and specialists from outside the school. When external specialists become involved, they should work closely with the teacher. Parents should be involved also and kept fully informed at every stage.

When there is a likelihood that the local authority will determine the special educational provision to be made for a pupil, a formal assessment must be conducted. Very detailed procedures are laid down for the conduct of such assessments. Parents must be involved in specified ways and have guaranteed rights of appeal. If the outcome of an assessment is that a child is deemed to require special educational provision, a formal Statement of Special Educational Needs must be made. This specifies the child's special educational needs and the provision that would be made to meet these needs. Statements must be reviewed every twelve months, and parents must be informed of any changes made.

Identifying children who may need special educational provision is the responsibility of local education authorities, but parents can initiate the process by requesting an assessment for their child; authorities must comply with this and arrange an assessment unless they consider it unreasonable. When a local authority decides to assess a child, it must inform the parents both of the intention to do so and how exactly it proposes to act.

In order to make an assessment, the authority must obtain educational, medical and psychological advice and 'any other advice which the authority considers desirable in the case in question'. The advice must be in written form and must relate to the child's present and likely future educational needs and how they are to be met. The requisite educational advice will be obtained, through the head teacher, from the child's class teachers in the case of a child at school. Medical advice will be obtained from the medical practitioner and psychological advice from an educational psychologist. These officers will normally be designated by the respective authorities for doing this work and should be familiar both with assessment practice and with local provision. Account must also be taken of any respresentations made by parents. These procedures are discussed in detail in a handbook produced by the Advisory Centre for Education (Newell, 1983).

INTEGRATION

Policy on integration in England and Wales is easy to state. Practice is more difficult to describe, not merely because of the usual gap between rhetoric and reality but because practice is so varied from authority to authority and even within authorities. As noted above, the Education Act 1981 gave a firm legislative commitment to integration: children with special educational needs should be educated in regular schools provided certain conditions were met, and when in a regular school they should engage in the activities of the school alongside other children to the greatest extent possible.

The legislation is backed by a broad consensus in favour of integration. Special schools have their advocates but they are outnumbered and probably feel beleaguered by the proponents of integration. Arguments against integration tend to focus on the present deficiencies of regular schools and their inability to cater for pupils with special educational needs. To that extent special schools are only defended as the lesser of two evils and, in principle at least, will no longer be necessary when regular schools have remedied their deficiencies.

The general support for integration has not, however, led to major changes in the use made of special schools. There has been a drop in absolute numbers but this reflects the decrease in the school-going population; the proportion of pupils attending special schools has not varied much over the past decade. This is due to a number of factors: the difficulties inherent in changing a long-established pattern of provision; limited progress in tackling the deficiencies of regular schools; and patterns of resource allocation.

Progress towards classroom integration has been more evident for some groups than for others. Pupils with physical or visual impairments have benefited most from the integration movement; pupils with moderate or severe learning difficulties have benefited considerably less; and pupils with emotional and behavioural difficulties are in fact experiencing greater segregation than before.

There are major differences between local education authorities in the use made of special schools and units attached to regular schools. Local policies are governed by past practices and resource allocation procedures, budgetary considerations and particular local factors. Some authorities are pursuing a policy of integrating into mainstream provision as many children with special needs as possible, whereas others are maintaining existing patterns of segregated provision.

The differences at local level are seen most clearly in the range of types of provision that are made. These can be illustrated by the following examples of practice, arranged roughly along a continuum from greater to lesser integration.

Pupils with special needs fitted into existing arrangements Pupils with special needs are allocated to classes on the same basis as other pupils, and all teachers are responsible for any pupils with special needs they happen to have in their classes. This avoids formalising the distinction between pupils with special needs and the others. However, it does require that all teachers be competent to teach pupils who have special educational needs; this can represent a considerable challenge for many schools and teachers.

Mainstream placement with specialist support provided within the class Pupils with special needs belong to the school's normal classes, usually at their local school, and receive all their teaching in them. They are not necessarily the sole responsibility of the class teacher, since specialist support of various kinds is available. The resources for support are decentralised and brought to the pupil and class teacher instead of being concentrated in one place so that pupils with special needs have to go to them. The requisite support can take various forms: an ancillary worker for a physically handicapped pupil; a speech therapist for a pupil with a language disorder.

Mainstream placement and withdrawal for specialist work Pupils with special needs belong to the school's normal classes and receive most of their teaching in them but are withdrawn for some specialist work, e.g. auditory training, specific therapies, teaching in particular areas. This support can be provided by a member of the school staff or by a visiting specialist. The essential difference between this arrangement and the previous one is in the location of the resources being utilised: in this case the pupil must leave his or her peers from time to time in order to go to the resources, whereas in the former the resources are brought to the pupil.

Mainstream placement, attending special class or unit part-time Pupils are registered with a mainstream group and receive some teaching there, but they also spend some of their teaching time in a segregated special class or unit. The teaching in the special class can be based on particular aspects of the curriculum, the same for all pupils in the special class, or it can be geared to providing flexible programmes for individual children.

Placement in a special class or unit, attending mainstream classes part-time Pupils are based in the special class and receive much of their teaching there but spend some time in mainstream classes as well. This form of organisation is regularly used for pupils with hearing impairments and those who have moderate learning difficulties. In many respects it appears identical to the previous arrangement. The critical difference is in the lines of responsibility for pupils and the resulting implications. When pupils are based in a special class or unit as distinct from a normal class group, they are likely to be perceived as different and to stand in a somewhat distant relationship to the rest of the school.

Full-time placement in a special class or unit Pupils attend a regular school but receive all their teaching in a special class or unit. This generally amounts to little more than locational integration.

Special school part-time, regular school part-time   Pupils spend part of their time in a special school, generally on its roll, and part of their time in a regular school. This entails the link schemes referred to above.

One of the most significant points to note about integration in England and Wales is the growing acceptance of integration as a matter of school reform, as opposed to the accumulation of individual programmes for particular pupils. As in most countries, the traditional view of special education based on a deficit model of handicap went unquestioned until the end of the seventies. When pupils' education was defined in terms of their handicaps, integration tended to be viewed as a matter of facilitating the placement of individual handicapped pupils in regular schools. As teachers and others came to realise that many pupils failed to learn because they were taught inappropriately, the deficit model of handicap gave way to an interactive model of special educational needs: learning success and failure are the result of an interaction between the individual's learning characteristics and factors in the learning environment, including school. This has led to a radically different view of integration. If schools are 'creating' learning difficulties, school reform is a prerequisite of integration. This reform has to encompass the entire school – curriculum, academic organisation, staffing, in-service training, whole-school relations.

7

THE NETHERLANDS

Cor J. W. Meijer

INTRODUCTION

The concept of special education in the Netherlands applies to a relatively large and separate school system. This school system comprises fifteen different types of schools of which the schools for the learning disabled and the schools for educable mentally retarded contain the highest proportion of children with special needs. Though much attention has been paid to the prevention of referrals to special education, the number of children in special education is still growing. Recently integration has become a central issue in Dutch policy making.

THE EDUCATIONAL SYSTEM

Structure

The Dutch educational system comprises the following types of education:

1 primary education (for children aged between 4 and 12);
2 primary and secondary special education for children who have special educational needs;
3 secondary education, which follows primary education, for pupils aged between 12 and 18 to 20. This exists in the following forms:
   — junior secondary vocational education
   — junior general secondary education
   — senior general secondary education
   — pre-university education

95

— senior secondary vocational education
— short senior secondary vocational courses
— part-time non-formal education for young people
— apprenticeship training;
4 higher education, for students aged 18 and over, which can be divided into:
— higher vocational education
— university education (inc. the Open University);
5 adult education.

(Ministerie van Onderwijs en Wetenschappen, 1989)

In the Netherlands school attendance is compulsory for all children aged 5–16. From the age of 16 there is a two-year part-time compulsory education phase.

The primary school phase (4–11/12 years) lasts eight years. Children generally attend school at the age of 4 though the compulsory phase starts at 5. In the first grades children receive about 750 hours of education annually, while in the higher grades 1,000 hours of education are given (circa 25 hours a week). A week consists of five school days. In special education similar regulations apply.

The educational system is characterised by homogeneous grouping. Children who do not master the educational matter may repeat a year. In this year-group system children have to deal with a fixed amount of educational material throughout the year. Generally, children (and their parents) receive a report containing information on their progress several times a year. These reports may serve as the basis of the decision to repeat a year or to pass to the next one.

The end of the primary school phase is characterised by tests (central examinations) in which the majority of the schools participate. This assessment procedure is crucial in the process of choosing the most adequate type of secondary education. After a relatively short transition period (one or two years) the students have to choose between the different types of secondary education. In the Netherlands this 'early streaming' system and a more comprehensive middle-school system coexist (the latter with a low frequency though). Recently the parliament has agreed to the implementation of a more general comprehensive school system with a common curriculum for the first three years of secondary education.

The main characteristics of the Dutch education system are the freedom of education and the centralised education policy. The threefold freedom – to found schools, to organise them and to determine on what religion or conviction they are based – is the reason for the wide variety of schools in the Netherlands (Ministerie van Onderwijs en Wetenschappen, 1989). There are two main categories of primary schools: denominational (65 per cent) and non-denominational (35 per cent). Under the terms of the Constitution, all schools are funded on an equal basis. This financial equality has produced an intricate complex of legislation and regulation. The variety of Dutch education can also be seen in the enormous number – 6,300 in all – of competent authorities. Each municipality is the competent authority for the publicly-run schools within its boundaries. The competent authority of denominational schools is the school board (ibid.).

Another distinctive feature of the Dutch education system is its centralised policy. Taking into account the provisions of the Constitution, central government controls education by means of legislation and regulations. It may do so directly by imposing qualitative or quantitative standards to be met by the educational process in schools and/or the outcomes in student progress, or indirectly by means of regulations concerning the financial and other resources schools receive from the government and the conditions schools must comply with, for example regarding the legal status of teachers (Ministerie van Onderwijs en Wetenschappen, 1989).

Support and guidance of schools in the Netherlands are taken care of by, among others, the school counselling services and the national educational advisory centres. The school counselling services mainly operate on the local and regional level. In general, they do not work on the basis of private, religious or ideological convictions, but serve all the schools in a certain area. They provide guidance to the school as a whole (system counselling) and they give support to individual pupils (pupil counselling). In addition they co-operate with the national educational advisory centres and/or specialised support institutions within the framework of certain projects. They also contribute to the implementation of in-service training programmes that are set up by the training institutes. The school counselling services are primarily focused on primary education and some types of special education. With regard to the latter they only offer system counselling (ibid.).

There are three national educational advisory centres: the Non-denominational Educational Advisory Centre, the Protestant Educational Advisory Centre and the Catholic Educational Advisory Centre. These three centres carry out activities at the national level in the fields of guidance and development, advice, information and evaluation, in particular with regard to secondary education. They do not counsel individual pupils but they do support schools. Moreover, they have a coordinating function in the realisation of the national innovation policy. Finally, they support the regional and local school counselling services (ibid.).

There are three further support institutions that operate at national level: the Institute for Educational Research, the National Institute for Educational Measurement and the National Institute for Curriculum Development.

Legislation

The first piece of educational legislation, the Elementary Education Act, was passed in 1801. However, it was the so-called 'Third Schools Act' of 1806 that contributed significantly to the improvement of education (Ministerie van Onderwijs en Wetenschappen, 1989). The Act provided for teaching qualifications, curriculum and inspection of schools. At that time public elementary schools were funded by the government and private schools were maintained from private sources (ibid.).

Religious political parties stressed the need for freedom of education and equal funding and this led to the Elementary Education Act of 1889 which provided for regulations concerning provisions for funds to denominational schools. In 1917 ('Pacification of 1917') equal funding of state and private education was finally laid down in the Constitution (ibid.). From 1920 on, the principle of financial equality was gradually extended to secondary and higher education, and nowadays there are nearly twice as many denominational schools as non-denominational ones.

Compulsory education came into force with the Compulsory Act of 1900. Schooling became compulsory between the ages of 7 and 12 years. In 1955 the Nursery Education Act came into force, though nursery education was still not compulsory (Ministerie van

Onderwijs en Wetenschappen, 1989). The present educational system for children aged 4–12 was implemented in 1985. The Primary Education Act of 1985 provided for the integration of nursery and primary education into 'new' primary schools and nowadays schooling is compulsory from the age of 5 onwards.

According to the law, teaching in primary schools aims at promoting emotional and intellectual development and creativity for each individual pupil. Besides knowledge acquisition, social, cultural and physical skills should be developed in an uninterrupted process. In the so-called 'school work plan' each school should provide an overall view of the school organisation and curriculum. In the Primary Education Act this school work plan is defined as the key instrument in the planning of teaching (ibid.).

SPECIAL NEEDS EDUCATION

Organisation

At the beginning of this century a small-scale system of special schools for various groups of children gradually emerged (Den Boer, 1990). Special education originally was regulated through special regulations under the heading of the Primary Act of 1920. In 1967 the so-called 'Special Education Decree', which specified the regulations for schools for special education, was issued. In 1985 this Decree was replaced by the Interim Act for Special Education and Secondary Special Education (ISOVSO). The Interim Act encompasses a period of ten years: in 1995 definitive legislation is envisaged. Recent integration discussions in the Netherlands make it difficult to predict whether or not a special education act will emerge in 1995.

'Special education' usually refers to the entire separate system of special education. This also includes the peripatetic supervision of a relatively small number of pupils in regular education (see below). Separate primary and secondary special education are intended for children for whom it has been established that a mainly orthopedagogical and orthodidactical approach is most appropriate.

Generally, the different types of (secondary) special education are classified into three categories. Group one consists of provision for the learning disabled (LOM schools), the educable mentally retarded (MLK schools) and children with developmental difficulties (IOBK departments).

Group two consists of provision for the following:

a deaf;
b hearing impaired;
c children with severe speech disorders;
d blind;
e partially sighted;
f physically handicapped;
g chronically ill;
h children in hospitals;
i severely maladjusted;
j multiply handicapped;
k children in schools attached to paedological institutes.

The paedological institutes are associated with a university.

Group three consists of only one type of school: the schools for severely mentally retarded children.

Generally, these fifteen types of provision for special education are located in a highly differentiated system of separate schools, though there are also departments that are attached to another type of special education (e.g. a department for children with severe speech disorders in a school for hearing impaired children). Provision for younger children with developmental difficulties (IOBK) may be located in departments attached to other school types for special education.

As has already been indicated, special education is intended for those pupils for whom it has been established that they are mainly dependent on an orthopedagogical and orthodidactical approach. Two comments must be made in this respect. First, the assessment that these pupils are dependent on a special approach is made by an admissions committee by means of the statutory admission examination. The second comment refers to the concept 'mainly orthopedagogical and orthodidactical approach'. This implies an approach that is difficult if not impossible to realise in regular education.

Education in special schools is based on a school work plan, which contains an overview of the organisation and content of education. The curriculum has to contain the same subjects that are taught in regular primary education. It is possible, however, to adjust the curriculum to children with multiple handicaps. Proposals to adjust the curriculum have to be submitted by the school board and approved by the Minister for Education and Science. The curriculum for severely mentally retarded children contains other subjects besides the curricula of other schools for special education. English and mathematics, for example, are not compulsory in these schools.

If necessary, use is made of an individual educational programme, in which it is indicated how the school work plan is elaborated for individual pupils or groups of pupils. In such a plan it has to be laid down which educational goals are aimed at for the specific pupil(s), in which way and by which means education will be organised, and when and how the results will be evaluated (Pijl and Blaauboer, 1990). On the basis of this evaluation the plan can be adjusted or remade. The new plan serves again as the guideline for education. A cycle like this may cover some months. In practice, many schools only develop individual educational programmes for pupils with serious or complicated problems (Pijl and Blaauboer, 1990).

The number of hours' education per day varies from 2.5 to 5.5. Special primary education is attended by pupils of the same age group as regular primary education. The age at which pupils are admitted varies: at some schools children are admitted at the age of 3, whereas the minimum age is 6 at other schools. Although the law does not set clear limits, pupils in secondary special education are admitted at the same age as in regular secondary education, namely 12 years. The maximum age is 20. Only in special cases can pupils attend the school above the age of 20.

After the child has been referred to the special school, an admissions committee – which usually consists of a psychologist, a physician, a social worker (not always) and the head teacher – decides whether the child can be admitted to the school for special education. Two years after the admittance, a re-examination has to take place in order to assess what results have been obtained in (the specific type of) education, in what way a further development of the pupil's capacities can be realised and whether the pupil should be transferred to regular education or to another type of special education.

The pupils who are found eligible for special education may or may not already have followed regular education for some years. Some pupils have not been able to follow regular education at the time of referral because of the severity of their handicap.

Recent developments

In the Netherlands there are about 1,000 separate schools for special education, of which two-thirds serve children who are learning disabled or educable mentally retarded.

The participation in special education varies according to handicap and age group. Overall, almost 5 per cent of all children in the primary age group participate in separate special education. In the secondary age group almost 4 per cent of all children attend secondary special schools. In Table 7.1 the percentages of children in special primary and secondary schools are listed according to type of handicap, age group and year. This table makes clear that the overall participation in the separate special schools is growing rapidly and that the schools for the educable mentally retarded and schools for the learning disabled represent the majority of children, both in primary and secondary schools.

There has been a remarkable growth in participation in separate special education the past few years. Although the absolute growth in the number of pupils is relatively small, there has been a considerable relative increase, given the large decline in the total number of children (Meijer, Pijl and Kramer, 1989). The growth is not equally strong in each type of school. Particularly in schools for the learning disabled the number of pupils has risen sharply.

The number of pupils from cultural minorities in special education has also increased (up to 11 per cent in 1990). Of course, these figures vary from region to region and from city to city.

In 1991, about 5 per cent of the total population in primary education attended separate special education, 2 per cent of whom were in schools for the learning disabled (LOM) and 1.5 per cent in schools for the educable mentally retarded (MLK). The other types of special education accounted for 1.5 per cent of the population.

During the past decade there has been a growing concern about the developments in special education. Not only the absolute size, but also the growth of the system as such is seen as alarming. As a result, government policy has been directed at reducing this

Table 7.1 The Netherlands: participation in special primary and special secondary education per type of school as a percentage of, respectively, the total number of pupils in elementary and special primary education combined and the total number of pupils in secondary and special secondary education combined

	1981 %	1985 %	1989 %
Younger children with devel. diff.	0.05	0.10	0.17
Primary special education	3.89	4.54	4.94
Deaf	0.07	0.04	0.03
Hearing impaired	0.08	0.09	0.09
Severe speech disorders	0.08	0.12	0.15
Blind	0.01	0.01	0.01
Partially sighted	0.02	0.01	0.01
Physically handicapped	0.15	0.11	0.10
Children in hospitals	0.00	0.05	0.04
Chronically ill	0.15	0.12	0.18
Educable mentally retarded	1.30	1.35	1.42
Severely mentally retarded	0.33	0.37	0.36
Severely maladjusted	0.15	0.16	0.17
Learning disabled	1.47	1.89	2.11
Paedological institutes	0.04	0.06	0.07
Multiply handicapped	0.05	0.16	0.19
Secondary special education	1.94	2.78	3.74
Deaf	0.02	0.03	0.04
Hearing impaired	0.06	0.08	0.10
Blind	0.01	0.01	0.01
Partially sighted	0.01	0.01	0.01
Physically handicapped	0.08	0.08	0.11
Children in hospitals	0.00	0.04	0.04
Chronically ill	0.03	0.02	0.05
Educable mentally retarded	0.93	1.17	1.43
Severely mentally retarded	0.21	0.23	0.32
Severely maladjusted	0.12	0.21	0.32
Learning disabled	0.45	0.88	1.27
Paedological institutes	0.01	0.01	0.01
Multiply handicapped	0.01	0.02	0.04

Source: Ministerie van Onderwijs en Wetenschappen, 1990

growth for a number of years now. In the following section some of these attempts will be discussed. In this context, the model of peripatetic supervision or ambulant teaching deserves special attention. By means of peripatetic teaching, pupils who are returned from special to regular education are entitled to certain facilities. The special education teacher can offer the regular education teacher and the pupil who is returned the support that is considered necessary for an adequate education in a regular school. These facilities are used to an increasing extent. Approximately 0.2 per cent of all pupils receive ambulant teaching. The pupils who are thus integrated are mainly between 12 and 17 years old. This arrangement also holds for pupils with special needs who, although they are eligible for special education, have not been referred to the separate educational system. The exact regulations and facilities are different for the various types of special education. Depending on the type of special school, the special school receives extra staff (Claessens *et al.*, 1989).

Formally, pupils are referred to special education by their parents. In practice, the regular education teacher often takes the initiative for a referral. The decision on referral and placement rests with the competent authorities. If the competent authorities refuse to admit a pupil, they inform the parents about the reason for this refusal in writing.

The competent authority of a public school is the town council. The competent authority of a denominational school is a legal body possessing legal rights that are, according to the statutes or regulations, aimed at offering education without making profits. There are about 1,000 schools for special education, of which 27 per cent are public and 73 per cent denominational. Approximately 20 per cent of all schools have a Protestant denomination, 30 per cent a Roman Catholic denomination and 20 per cent are founded on the basis of other convictions. All schools are funded by the government on an equal basis.

INTEGRATION

Government policy

In the past decade integration policy has been primarily focused on improving the diagnostic and remedial skills of teachers in elementary education. For this purpose several projects have been initiated. These have been concerned with co-operation between special and regular education and the transfer of knowledge to regular education by offering courses to regular education teachers. The expectation was that this policy would lead to adequate education for as many pupils as possible in regular education. Moreover, the number of referrals to special education was expected to diminish through these measures. Consequently, integration is often defined in terms of mainstreaming: the extension and intensification of measures and activities, especially at group and school level, for the purpose of a pupil care that is as intensive as possible, in particular for those who show specific needs. In doing so, specific goals and interim goals that are defined by the school have to be attained in a certain amount of time (ARBO, 1984) (ARBO = Advisory Council for Primary and Special Education). Despite the legislation, facilities and projects, this policy has not yet offered many positive results. The statistics even show that the number of referrals to special education continues to rise.

As has been mentioned before, the growth of special education can be mainly explained by the rise in the number of learning disabled pupils. It seems as if Dutch schools for regular education have grown accustomed to solving their problems by referring pupils to special education. These developments are watched with great concern by the government as well as many educationalists. There is a general wish to implement the integration policy in practice. In particular, parent organisations from the so-called 'group two' and 'group three' schools (see p. 100 above) do have an explicit integration policy. Parent organisations for the learning disabled, however, doubt the possibility of integrating these pupils under the present circumstances. They think regular education is not yet capable of catering for these pupils and they are afraid that integration will exacerbate the problems.

The above-mentioned problems have resulted in a change of policy by the Dutch Ministry for Education and Science, which is published in a report called 'Weer samen naar school' ('Together to school again') (Ministerie van Onderwijs en Wetenschappen, 1990). In this report an analysis is made of the factors that have contributed to the growth of special education. Educational factors, system characteristics and policy factors seem relevant to this problem. Children differ and these differences seem to increase. Schools are not able to deal with these growing differences. As a result more and more children end up in the danger zone. Despite all the educational innovations of the past decades, it is clear that education mainly focuses on the average pupil. If there are too many pupils with specific needs in the classroom, teaching becomes a complex problem.

To solve the above-mentioned problem, teachers need support. The support that is available is located outside the school building: in schools for special education, school counselling services and similar support institutions. There is not enough support in the school itself. The only way out for teachers is to refer children with specific needs to schools that have more time and expertise available: the separate schools for special education (Ministerie van Onderwijs en Wetenschappen, 1990).

Special and regular education work independently and it is this system aspect, among other things, which stimulates referral to special education. For special help is only available when pupils enter a school for special education. Even if temporary support could provide a solution, it is impossible in practice. Legal obstacles make it difficult for the two separate school systems to organise this support in a more flexible way. This means that the pupil with special needs has to be taken to the facilities instead of vice versa. The responsibility for the pupil is passed on to another part of the educational system (ibid.).

It must be said that special education is an attractive alternative: it offers special provision for pupils with special needs. It is the system itself that deprives regular education of the possibility of helping pupils under the same conditions. In this sense, the provision enhances the need (the law of supply and demand). It is difficult to realise collaboration between regular and special education, because each school has its own financial, administrative and staff systems. Introducing additional provision, and decision making in general, are matters for the individual school. There is no network in which a larger variety of experience, expertise and facilities is available (ibid.).

The fact that the legal regulations of the past decades have not resulted in a solution of the problem has to do with policy-making characteristics as well as with the specific effects of the regulations themselves. The wish to cater for a wider range of educational needs in regular schools (mainstreaming) has resulted in numerous regulations concerning pupils with special needs. As a consequence, means and facilities are only available under strict conditions, which makes it difficult to use them flexibly. This has caused a situation in which the teacher responsible, that is the regular education teacher, has no influence on the allocation of the resources that are available for children with special needs (ibid.).

In the report 'Together to school again' the Dutch government investigates the possibility of regional co-operation between special and regular schools in the same organisational unit. Such a unit would comprise a number of regular schools together with a school for learning disabled or a school for educable mentally retarded. Each unit would have responsibility for the education of *circa* 2,000 pupils (regular and special pupils) and be autonomous in the use of resources within the statutory regulations. In some regions this co-operation has already been put into practice, though not at the level of autonomy that the report proposes. Recently, organisations in the field of education (parent organisations, organisations of school boards and staff organisations) have approved the main lines of this policy. In 1991 the parliament agreed the main features of the policy. The Dutch government finances the institution of the regional co-operation units. In addition, it is intended that further co-operation units will be set up between 1991 and 1995 and that these units will start to function according to the goals that were set: the integration of pupils with special needs in regular education with the aid of teachers and other experts from special education.

The Dutch government asked the Advisory Council for Primary and Special Education (ARBO) in 1991 to give advice on the integration possibilities of the so-called 'group two' schools. In July 1991 the ARBO proposed to continue the stimulation of integration and to simplify the classification of school types. This should take place without losing the expertise and knowledge of special education. It is still unclear when and how this policy will be implemented.

Integration experiences

Integration in the Netherlands can be described from different angles. A possible starting point is government measures, such as the aforementioned peripatetic supervision (or ambulant teaching), in-service training of teachers and more or less local experiments aimed at bringing special and regular education more closely together. An alternative point of view is to consider developments in the field of education independently of government policy. For example, this might entail a focus on developments with regard to the integration of children with Down's syndrome in regular education. Particularly through pressure of parental movements, more and more of these children are catered for by regular education. It is also possible to point at local initiatives that – apart from the government funded projects – strive for integration. In this section, however, attention is given primarily to the first of these perspectives, the government measures.

Regarding peripatetic supervision, Claessens *et al.* (1989) conclude that it is not possible to make statements on the effectiveness of peripatetic supervision or on its importance in relation to other policy measures in this field. The results of this study do indicate, however, that peripatetic supervision can be a valuable instrument for improving the relationship between special and regular education. Contacts between the two types of school become more intensive, and through co-operation and the way in which consultation takes place schools learn to know each other better. As a result, schools have a positive attitude to peripatetic supervision.

There are, of course, a number of problems with regard to this legislation, such as lack of time, insufficient opportunities for consultation and the restricted possibilities to support pupils with problems. The peripatetic teachers themselves have problems concerning a lack of clarity with regard to their function and tasks. Moreover, peripatetic supervision is often an occasional phenomenon, particularly in elementary education. This is related to the fact that only a small number of schools have more than one pupil receiving peripatetic supervision (ibid.).

In 1988, almost 5,000 pupils received ambulant teaching, the majority (75 per cent) of them in secondary education. Schools for children with sensory handicaps in particular make use of this facility. It should also be mentioned that, since the measure was introduced in 1985, the number of pupils who received ambulant teaching has doubled (ibid.). This growth can be considered indicative of the fact that the principal aim of peripatetic supervision has been attained. This is to stimulate the placement of pupils in regular education who, without this measure, would have to rely upon the separate system of special education. At the same time it should be noticed that peripatetic supervision has not led to a decrease in the number of pupils in the separate special educational system.

In summary, it can be stated with regard to peripatetic supervision that schools make use of the facilities offered to an increasing extent. However, it is not known what long-term effects this measure will produce. Moreover, as has already been mentioned, there has not been an assessment of effects in practice. An important problem is that the two largest types of special education, i.e. the schools for learning disabled and educable mentally retarded children, make use of peripatetic supervision only to a minimal degree. From these types of schools, which are important target groups of the government's mainstreaming policy, very few pupils return to regular schools (Claessens, 1990). So, although peripatetic supervision is increasingly available, it does not reach the target group it is meant for.

The second policy measure to be discussed here is the in-service training of teachers. Within the framework of the integration policy, approximately 25,000 teachers in elementary education followed courses in reading during the period 1985–8. The first course started in 1985/6 and ran for over three years. In addition, extra attention was paid to providing information on reading instruction, reading problems and the guidance of schools with regard to reading (Vinjé, 1990). This mainstreaming policy was focused on reading readiness, beginning reading and decoding. The national educational advisory centres distributed materials, which they expounded at regional meetings for teachers from the teacher training courses and counsellors from the school counselling services (Stokking, 1990). This mainly concerned materials relating to differentiation, individualisation and/or remediation in beginning reading instruction that were used by the schools (ibid.).

The in-service training operation has been the subject of two studies (Stokking, 1990 and Vinjé, 1990). The results of these evaluations can be summarised as follows: at this moment, there is no evidence of a positive effect of this policy on the reading attainments of pupils. The in-service training has not resulted in an improvement of reading performance (Vinjé, 1990). It seems, however, that a small improvement has been established in decoding, reading comprehension and spelling skills (ibid.). It is likely, however, that this improvement has to be ascribed to other factors (ibid.), since no differences have been found between teachers who participated and teachers who did not.

A third important pillar of the government policy is the so-called projects policy. By means of extra personnel and material facilities, certain innovations can be tested out on a small scale. During the past ten years a number of projects have been carried out in different policy fields, such as projects aimed at a more intensive co-operation between regular and special education, projects aimed at thematic subjects such as referral and admission/placement, and projects dealing with returning pupils from special to regular education.

In the past few years several evaluations of the projects policy have been carried out, which will not all be discussed in detail here. In summary, it can be concluded that in these projects regular and special schools have been able to learn about each other's methods and approaches. Moreover, there has been a transfer of knowledge between the two types of education, which has also resulted in the actual use of certain procedures and strategies. In some elementary schools initial steps have been made to realise further mainstreaming (Kool and Wolfgram, 1987). A decrease in the number of referrals from regular to special education has not yet been observed, neither in general nor with the schools that participated in these projects.

Six of these projects have been continued within the framework of the European Community (the so-called HELIOS progamme). These are projects aimed at a closer co-operation between regular and special education with the purpose of improving the quality of regular education. This should result in a reduction of the number of referrals to special education. Another project within the framework of the HELIOS programme is carried out in the city of Rotterdam. The aim of this project is to reduce referral rates to special education by setting up a support system in regular education, by using special education as a temporary provision and by stimulating the return of pupils from regular to special education. Naturally, the activities in the local projects are determined by local circumstances. Each project, however, involves at least one special school which co-operates closely with ten to twenty regular education schools. In this sense, it concerns networks that fit within the policy of the Dutch government. In the projects different innovation approaches are applied, such as training individual teachers or having schools collaborate to implement a certain innovation. The communication between regular and special education is realised by means of workshops, discussions, consultation and in-service training of teachers. Also, materials and procedures are developed: screening tests, consultation procedures, co-operation, special classes, counselling, registration procedures, special education pupils following parts of regular education. The question now is: what changes occur in the projects?

As regards the attitude of parents and teachers the projects report a positive change. Through more intensive information transfer to the parents, negative labelling of children is prevented. Parents are positive about children staying in regular education instead of being referred to special education. Teachers too show a positive attitude towards the idea of integration. Consultation with the special education teacher enhances their self-confidence. With regard to the changes at school, the projects report an increase in teacher skills. Moreover, teachers have learnt to look beyond the scope of their own subject, class or school. The projects also mention more attention to individual pupil counselling and the team meetings where the pupils are discussed. Instead of the general standard procedure a more differentiated approach is chosen. Apart from this, the projects also report more mutual support. In summary, the projects report an increase in the professionalism of regular education.

As regards changes at pupil level, the following results can be mentioned. First, more pupils can stay in regular education through the projects than without these facilities. It is reported that the majority of pupils who are eligible for special education remain in regular education. Generally, the pupils keep up well, thanks to a proper preparation. Moreover, the projects report that the pupils who stay gain in self-confidence and have a positive self-image. The negative labelling of these pupils disappears through planning joint activities for pupils from regular and special education.

The attitude of regular schools towards integration is positive; they are prepared to continue to move along the route they have taken. According to some, however, much depends on the amount of time and facilities available. The regular schools should have

111

sufficient resources to be able to translate the idea of integration into practice.

It should be emphasised that the above-mentioned changes and experiences were reported by the projects themselves, and that they are not findings of an independent scientific study. Such research has not yet been conducted.

Problems in integration development

In the preceding sections we have mentioned the problems that have been identified in the educational field and by educational policy. The fact that the two educational systems, i.e. regular and special education, are separate, is one of the biggest problems in the integration process in the Netherlands. At all levels this distinction is present: financing, legislation, teacher training and so on. It is this separation the Dutch government wants to tackle.

In terms of costs per pupil, special education is much more expensive than regular education. In 1989 the costs for an average special education pupil were four times as high as the costs for a regular education pupil. This varied from two and a half times as high (learning problems) to seven times as high (multiply handicapped). It is obvious that expenditure on special education in the Netherlands is relatively high. The financing system, however, inhibits integration. The two educational systems are financed independently, so there are no incentives for regular education to spend extra time and attention on pupils with special needs. On the contrary, the financing system makes it attractive to refer pupils to special education. Moreover, the amount of time allocated to teachers and other experts in special education depends on the number of pupils in the school for special education. This can be considered an incentive for admission to special education. In addition, special education is not motivated to refer pupils back to regular education either. Although this has been changed somewhat by the introduction of peripatetic supervision, it is still unattractive to return large numbers of children to regular education. Generally speaking, schools lack inducements to pursue an integration policy. Recent government policy with regard to schools for the learning disabled and for the educable mentally retarded (as has been described earlier in this chapter) is meant to be a first step to remove the problems mentioned above.

8

ANALYSIS OF FINDINGS

Sip Jan Pijl and Cor J. W. Meijer

SUMMARY OF COUNTRY DESCRIPTIONS

Italy

Since 1977 special and regular education have in principle been fully integrated. In a regular classroom of twenty students no more than two students with special needs may be placed. The regular teacher who teaches students with special needs is assisted by a support teacher. Support is provided for students with special needs on a one-to-four ratio. Before additional support is made available, the student is examined by a multi-disciplinary team in order to determine the kind of support that is needed. This results in the issuing of a certificate. According to figures from the Italian Ministry of Education, the percentage of students with special needs integrated in regular classrooms is almost 100 per cent. In addition, there is a small number of separate special schools for mentally and/or sensorily handicapped students.

Some authors report problems in the implementation of integration. The reason for these problems is that regular teachers do not always regard the instruction of students with special needs as their responsibility. The fact that in Italy most children are in ordinary schools does not imply that all are integrated in a curricular sense. Because of the lack of evaluation research on this issue little is in fact known about the degree to which integration has been achieved. Nevertheless, integration in Italy is a widespread phenomenon and, in spite of implementation problems, it is supported by society at large.

113

Denmark

Characteristic features of the Danish educational system are decentralisation, integration and normalisation. The effort to achieve integration of handicapped students in education and the willingness to let handicapped people grow up in their own environment, have resulted in the placement of large numbers of students with special needs in regular education. The facilities for students with special needs in the Folkeskole are extremely varied: a special teacher who is present part-time in the regular classroom to assist individual children and/or groups; part-time instruction in a well-equipped, special classroom (the clinic); instruction in an intensive course of several months; full-time special classroom. A multi-disciplinary team decides on the provision of these services to students.

Outside the Folkeskole a number of special services are available to students with special needs: a special school, a special school and a regular school operating as 'twins', and centres for special education, which are often attached to a regular school (so-called centre classes).

Danish education is considered by many as progressive because of its far-reaching integration of regular and special education. Important factors contributing to its success are: the homogeneity of the Danish society, the close and long-lasting bonds between teacher and students, the relaxed atmosphere in schools and the wide acceptance of being labelled 'special' for a while.

Sweden

Although the instruction of students in segregated settings conflicts with Swedish educational policy, a limited number of special schools exist. Most of them are due to integrate in the near future, i.e. they will become special classes in a regular 'Grundskola'. For students referred to special schools an assessment procedure is compulsory.

Quite a number of mentally retarded students are placed in special classes within the regular school. Because it is not the local community but the region that is responsible for this particular group, a registration procedure is necessary. The special teachers in the special classes are paid by the regional authorities; they have their own head teacher and use their own methods and materials. In practice this tends to lead to special schools within the regular school, especially in the larger schools.

More advanced forms of integration are found in the working unit. Working units consist of three to four classes of approximately the same grade. The members of the working unit are the regular teachers, a special teacher and – depending on the type of students in the unit – additional staff. A special teacher can be attached to a working unit without the students needing to be labelled as handicapped.

The working unit can offer a wide array of organisational approaches: teachers can instruct students individually or in small groups within the classroom; a class can be split up for certain subjects; intensive small group instruction can be arranged outside the classroom; students can follow instruction in a lower grade class, and so on.

Swedish informants state that there are serious difficulties in integrating students with special needs into regular education. In quite a number of schools separate special groups are formed under the responsibility of the special education teacher within the working unit structure. This is often easy to realise: four classes will provide enough special needs children to set up a full-time special class.

United States

Traditionally the United States is regarded as one of the countries that has made a great deal of progress in the integration of regular and special education. The array of placement options available to children with special needs in the United States encompasses, among other things, self-contained classrooms, resource rooms, itinerant teachers and in-class services. Students with special needs can be placed in the self-contained classroom full-time (a special classroom in a regular school), can go part-time to a resource room (also a special classroom in a regular school) or receive support from a special teacher, individually or within a group, inside or outside the regular classroom. Students are eligible for help, in any setting, as soon as placement decisions have been made on the basis of an assessment procedure.

In principle, the regular teacher takes care of instruction in the regular class, while the special teacher is responsible for the pull-out parts of the programme. The two groups of teachers operate rather independently of one another. This separation hinders integration and is reinforced by the differences in funding, training, experience and perceived roles in education of both regular and special teachers.

In the last few years the education community in the United States has been deeply involved in what is called the Regular Education Initiative (REI). The basic idea in this revival of the integration movement is that regular education ought to take full responsibility for students with special needs and that special education should serve as a resource for regular education. Recently a series of projects has started in which the basic ideas of the REI are being implemented in various ways.

England and Wales

Major changes to the law on special education were introduced in 1981. Children were no longer regarded as handicapped but as having special educational needs. The law also has a clear presumption in favour of integration: pupils with special educational needs should attend regular schools and be educated alongside peers unless there are specific reasons to the contrary.

The legislation sets out procedures for identifying children with special educational needs and conducting assessments to establish what their needs actually are. Very detailed procedures are laid down for conducting formal assessments where they are judged to be necessary. If the outcome of an assessment is that a child is deemed to require special educational provision, a formal statement of special educational needs must be made. This specifies the child's educational needs and the provision that should be made to meet these needs.

Special educational provision for other pupils takes the form of special classes in regular schools or, more commonly, modifications to mainstream educational provision. Special education is supported by a number of services external to the school. These are usually the responsibility of the local education authority. The most important source of support is the learning support service; its principal function is to assist regular schools in the task of educating pupils with learning difficulties. Staff from the services spend much of their time in schools, teaching pupils and advising teachers. Most local education authorities operate specialist peripatetic services for pupils with hearing impairments and visual impairments.

The Netherlands

Special education in the Netherlands is provided in fifteen different types of schools with approximately 100,000 students. Seventy per cent of the special students in special education go to schools for learning disabled or educable mentally retarded students. In the last five years a growing number of students with special needs have returned to regular education; this has been made possible by a support model known as 'ambulante begeleiding' – a visiting special teacher model. Approximately 0.2 per cent of all children are thus integrated, most of whom are 12 to 17 years old.

In the Netherlands much attention has been paid to the prevention of special education referrals. Regular education teachers were enabled to follow additional training, new materials were developed and additional services were offered to regular schools. In quite a number of projects the co-operation between schools for special education and schools for regular education is enhanced.

Since the number of children in special education is still growing, the effectiveness of the projects and training is presumably low. Recently integration has become a major component of educational reform policy. The integration of special needs children should be the result of setting up networks of co-operating regular and special schools.

QUANTITATIVE ASPECTS OF INTEGRATION

Comparing countries on statistics is difficult. Comparability is threatened by differences in definitions of the special needs group, in drop-out figures, in regulations with respect to counting minority groups or students with a low socio-economic status and so on. Furthermore, the information presented here represents the state of play regarding integration at one point in time, and further developments may have taken place in the intervening period.

By using Kobi's descriptive framework we have tried to establish the percentages of integrated and segregated special needs children in the six countries (Pijl and Meijer, 1991, 1992). In our definition we regard as segregation every educational setting that does not allow social contacts between children with special needs and their peers (special schools, permanent special classes).

In Table 8.1 the total numbers of registered special needs children in the six countries are given in three main categories. By registration we mean the formal procedures that are used to define a child as having special needs, independent of the educational setting (special school, special class, resource room, regular school).

Table 8.1 Number of students registered as having special needs as a percentage of the total population aged 6 to 17

Registration		Countries
Low:	0–3 %	Italy, England and Wales, Sweden
Medium:	4–7 %	The Netherlands
High:	>8 %	USA, Denmark

It is clear that countries differ in the degree to which they formally register students with special needs. These differences not only reflect general registration policies and societal mores but they also result from legislative requirements and financial regulations. Countries with high levels of registration are the United States and Denmark. They register respectively about 9 and 13 per cent of all children as having special needs. Italy, Sweden and England and Wales register only a relatively small number of students. The Netherlands takes an intermediate position.

In Table 8.2 the percentages of children in the segregated provisions are listed. The two ends of the 'segregation continuum' are Italy, with officially almost no segregated children, and the Netherlands, with approximately 4 per cent of children in segregated provision.

If we take into account the qualitative information in the country descriptions it appears that the six countries can be divided into three broad categories. These represent three different policy options.

Table 8.2 Number of segregated special needs students as a percentage
of the total population aged 6 to 17

Segregation		Countries
Low:	0–1 %	Italy, Sweden
Medium:	1–2 %	England and Wales, USA, Denmark
High:	>2 %	The Netherlands

— The first policy can be described as a one-track integration policy. This refers to the emphasis these countries lay on non-segregation, a policy which is mainly oriented towards regular education as far as the serving of children with special needs is concerned. Italy and Sweden are clear representatives of this 'one-track policy', which can be characterised as avoiding segregation by all means and as having a policy of low registration.
— The second group of countries operate a 'two-track' system. The Netherlands (and other West European countries such as Germany and Belgium) segregate a group of special needs students in a special school system that is quite large. The two school systems work more or less separately and independently. There are some innovations in the direction of integration but these are encompassed within the two-track policy. The separate system of special education plays a key role in the integration efforts, and policy in these two-track countries is oriented towards both special and regular education. Separate laws for both systems are indicative of this two-track philosophy.
— The third group is characterised by 'multi-track' policies. These countries offer a flexible system of education to special needs children. Denmark, England and Wales, and the United States offer a continuum of services for special needs students. Denmark and the United States also register a high number of students. There is a pragmatic need for doing so; registration means financial support whether in separate or integrated settings.

The figures presented here and our conclusions on the three policy approaches give some impression of the situation regarding integration in the six countries. When we look at these figures, the question arises: to what extent can integration be judged as successful? This is a very difficult question to answer. Successful in what respect? To whom? By what criteria? How assessed? By whom? Allowing for some uncertainty, we can make some general comments on the quality of integration, using our conceptual model.

First of all, it is clear that countries differ in the extent to which they segregate children with special needs. They also differ in the way the continuum of provision is built up, its range and the number of possible positions on the continuum. Moreover, the distribution of children along the continuum varies between and within countries.

If we regard curricular integration (i.e. the participation of children with special needs in core activities of the curriculum alongside peers) as the highest level of integration in the school and look at practice in the six countries, then it can be concluded that these countries seem to 'agree' that approximately 1 to 1.5 per cent of all children are difficult to integrate on a curricular level in regular education. They succeed in integrating a large proportion of this group physically and socially but have major problems with integrating them in a curricular way (Pijl and Meijer, 1991). They stay in separate groups for a large part of the school day and do not share curricular activities with non-handicapped peers.

'One-track' countries like Italy and Sweden with a very low proportion of children in separate special education settings also experience major difficulties in bringing about curricular integration (Pijl and Meijer, 1991). This does not mean that their practice should be regarded as unsuccessful. On the contrary, they succeed in the social integration of a group of children that cannot be dealt with in regular settings in many other countries. However, this must not be regarded as curricular integration (Pijl and Meijer, 1992).

QUALITATIVE ASPECTS OF INTEGRATION

One thing becomes immediately clear from the integration practices outlined above: there is no such thing as the integration of regular and special education. There is an enormous diversity between as well as within the countries in the way integration is given shape. The factors behind this diversity are as varied as integration itself, for instance: history, societal convictions, financial resources, types of handicap distinguished and population density. For example, teacher attitudes towards students with special needs in Sweden are strongly influenced by the social democratic ideology; in Denmark by the generally accepted drive for normalisation; in the Netherlands by the availability of separate special schools all over the country (due in part to the high population density); and in the United States by a strict division of responsibilities between regular and special teachers. Another factor is the mode of implementation: the Italian revolution in psychiatry has had a large impact on thinking about separate forms of education and resulted in a sweeping and rapid transformation of the education of students with special needs, while in countries like Sweden or England and Wales it has been (indeed could not have been otherwise) a step-by-step process taking decades. These differences make the transfer of practice from one country to another extremely problematic. In the following we address a number of issues relating to the responsibility for education, the labelling process and the educational system.

Our first conclusion is that the placement of students with special needs in regular education settings will not succeed unless it is clear that the regular teacher is responsible for students with special needs who are placed part-time in special settings. The regular teacher has to coordinate the educational offerings for the students with special needs both in regular and special settings and should be willing to take a final responsibility for these students. Of course, the other teachers involved have to stay in close contact with the coordinating teacher, otherwise, two different educational programmes are created within the school, which is shown in particular by the situation in the United States: one within the regular and one within the special setting. This can easily result in the fragmentation of instruction. This situation is more likely to occur in those countries where regular and special teachers operate in separate organisational frameworks with, among other things, their own head teachers, materials, teacher training programmes and salary structures. Restating responsibilities, therefore, also bears upon organisational/administrative structures in education.

In most countries the provision of special services to handicapped students is dependent on a 'statement', a 'label', a 'certificate' or an 'admission procedure'. Normally such a procedure is a formality for students with easily recognised handicaps (e.g. blindness, physical handicaps). This does not hold for students with learning disabilities, mild mental retardation and/or emotional disturbances. Almost every time a (regular) teacher proposes a student from one of the latter groups for a labelling procedure, the outcome of that procedure supports segregation. This reinforces for all concerned – the regular teachers, the student, the parents – the idea that the student in question has special problems and needs special measures. It is very difficult to convince those involved that these problems can be dealt with adequately in a regular education setting: after all, the student's problems came to light in this particular setting and the regular teacher was unable to cope with them. So, the labelling process hampers integration attempts and adds to the segregation of students. Securing additional finances for special support is often the most important reason for such a labelling process. A different procedure for the provision of special services could lessen the need to label students as 'special' or 'deviant'. Swedish administrative procedures illustrate how this can be done. A working unit comprises regular and special services that are partly independent of the number of students with special needs. Also worth mentioning in this respect is the Danish model, which tends to the other extreme. In Denmark special services are provided – and discontinued – relatively easily, and so many students receive these services for short periods that the label is of less significance there.

The effort towards less segregated education for handicapped students has been elaborated in the founding of full-time special classes within or closely associated with regular schools (for instance Denmark, Sweden and the United States). Sometimes special classes within the regular schools arise without having been intended in the policy framework (for instance in Italy and a part of the working units in Sweden). In general, the effects in terms of integration of special classes in regular schools do not look too promising: students with special needs stick together and do not play and talk with other students, both groups follow instructions together for only a limited number of hours and even teachers stay apart (see for instance the descriptions of Sweden and the United States). Establishing special classes in regular schools is not always an integrative measure; it may even lead to an increase of segregation. Special classes in this sense should be limited in time (for instance no more than 60 per cent of the school time) and be focused on part of the subject matter (for instance reading, writing and arithmetic).

In summary, the factors making an important contribution to a successful integration of students with special needs in regular education are:

— regular teachers having the final responsibility for the education of handicapped students in both regular and special settings;
— the avoidance of formal labelling procedures as the means of funding special services;
— a limit on the amount of time spent in special classes and the number of subjects taught in special classes in regular schools.

In our view these factors are essential for the long-term success of integration policy. But, of course, the success of integration is not only determined by policies. It has to be implemented in the regular classroom and the regular teacher may feel unable or unwilling to deal with children with special needs. In the next chapter the role of the teacher will be addressed and a closer look will be taken at the teacher variables relevant to integration.

9

INTEGRATION AND THE TEACHER

Seamus Hegarty

INTRODUCTION

Integration is in the end a matter of providing appropriate, high quality education for pupils with special needs in regular schools. Whether or not this happens depends critically on teacher variables, specifically their willingness to take on this task and their ability to do so. These two variables are interconnected: teachers, like others, are more willing to carry out tasks for which they have the requisite skills and resources; and the possession of a repertoire of skills likewise engenders the desire to use them. More generally, however, these variables are dependent on other factors. It is possible to discern specific country differences in relation to these factors, and this chapter outlines some of these.

Integration does not of course depend just on teacher variables, and some of these other factors could be considered in their own right. It is instructive, however, to consider them primarily through their impact on teachers. School reform – and in most countries integration is best seen as a matter of school reform – depends critically on the teacher force, and is most likely to be effective when the dynamics of teacher variables are well understood.

TEACHER ATTITUDES

Teachers' attitudes to disability, and more specifically their willingness to teach pupils with special needs, depend on many factors. Three are singled out for consideration here: the nature of the society; prevailing conceptions of disability and learning difficulty; and school financing mechanisms.

The first of these is exceedingly general, and it can be difficult to draw explicit links between the nature of a society and teachers' attitudes. There are some pointers, however. Sweden's social democratic ideology has had a strong influence on education policy and provides a natural context for integration. In such a society, as in Denmark, where the principles of normalisation have gained widespread acceptance, teachers are more likely to be positively disposed towards integration and to accept the presence of pupils with special needs in the regular school as part of the normal state of affairs. In Italy, the radical change in the direction of special educational provision – from special schooling to near-total integration – grew out of shifts in public opinion regarding deinstitutionalisation in health care and psychiatric provision and decentralisation of public services.

There has been a major shift in the understanding of the nature of learning difficulties over the past twenty years. The traditional view was that some children were defective in various ways, had handicaps, and as a result were unable to learn in the same way as normal children. Being handicapped, they needed special teaching quite different from the teaching required by other children. It made administrative and pedagogic sense to provide this teaching in separate establishments. Moreover, within this handicapped group children could be grouped further into separate categories – blind, mentally handicapped, learning disabled and so on – so that schools of different kinds could be fashioned to meet the needs of particular groups in a more targeted way. The result of adopting this view of learning difficulties was a framework for assessment and provision that has lasted for many years and has been instrumental in expanding the amount and sophistication of services for pupils designated as handicapped.

This traditional view has been sharply challenged by an alternative view which sees children's learning difficulties at school as deriving from the interaction between innate factors and environmental factors. Among the latter the regular school itself is coming to be viewed as a major source of learning difficulties. Inappropriate curriculum content and teaching methods, insensitive handling and an over-competitive school ethos, can add up to an utter failure to meet the individual needs of particular children, with the result that they fail to learn and become candidates for segregated schooling.

126

There are large differences between countries, and even within them, in the extent to which the traditional view of child defect or the alternative, interactive view is dominant. It seems reasonable to suppose that teachers are more likely to regard special schools as the natural place for pupils with learning difficulties where the traditional view holds sway, and that there will be less integration as a result. Some support for this can be obtained by contrasting the Netherlands with England and Wales. Dutch legislation and administrative arrangements are strongly predicated on the existence of a large number of distinct categories of handicap, defined in the traditional, non-educational way. Legislation in England and Wales, by contrast, has eschewed the notion of categories of handicap since 1981 and describes the target group in terms of 'special educational needs' – a tacit acknowledgement of the interactive notion of learning difficulties. While there are undoubtedly other factors at play, this difference may be one of the reasons why the Netherlands has approximately three times as many of its pupils in special schools as England and Wales.

The way in which schools are financed can affect teachers' receptivity to pupils with special needs. The latter generally require more resources – of time and materials – than other pupils, sometimes, as in the case of deaf pupils or those with severe learning difficulties, substantially more. If regular schools are not resourced accordingly when they take on the education of these pupils, it is extremely difficult to build up positive attitudes on the part of teachers or to sustain them over a period of time.

Denmark, Italy and Sweden, which are all characterised by relatively high levels of integration, also have resource allocation systems which are conducive to evoking positive teacher attitudes. Thus, in Italy, a class containing a handicapped pupil may not have more than twenty pupils in total, and no class may have more than two handicapped pupils. In the Netherlands, by contrast, the funding mechanism is considered to inhibit integration: resources are targeted on pupils in special schools and do not readily follow them into regular schools. Apart from making integration more difficult to achieve, this also means that teachers in regular schools are less likely to be receptive to having pupils with special needs in their schools. England and Wales is an interesting intermediate case where efforts are currently being made to target the resources on the child, via a Statement of Special Educational Needs, with the intention that the resources will follow the child regardless of placement. It will be instructive to see how effectively this works and what impact it will have on teacher attitudes.

TEACHER ABILITIES

Positive attitudes and willing teachers are not enough; as the old proverb recognises, the road to hell is paved with good intentions. Teachers must be able to deliver an education of high quality, differentiated according to individual need. Again, there are numerous factors that impinge on this. Three will be considered here: teacher competence, support and the curriculum.

Initial teacher training is the starting point. In most countries nowadays initial training follows a common pattern for all teachers regardless of whether or not they are likely to work with pupils with special needs in their future careers. Some training courses offer options on aspects of special education which help to prepare some teachers for teaching pupils with learning difficulties, but only a minority ensure that all trainee teachers are introduced to the fundamentals of special educational needs. Since 1989 in England and Wales all students in training have been 'expected to have acquired a range of teaching strategies and skills suitable for a wide ability range and be able to identify pupils with special educational needs'.

This failure to provide some coverage of special needs for all teachers in initial training is a major drawback to promoting integration. If the aim is to give class teachers responsibility, albeit with appropriate support, for pupils with special needs, it has to be assumed that all teachers will throughout their careers find themselves taking on such responsibility. In other words, it becomes an essential component of the job, not an optional add-on for some teachers. It should therefore be encompassed by initial teacher training, as part of the core material covered by all trainees.

Given the limitations of initial teacher training, the focus shifts to in-service training and the on-going professional development of teachers. Integration is one kind of school reform and like all such reforms requires shifts in attitude, school organisation and teaching practice. Appropriate in-service training is a key ingredient in this process. It can speed up developments, help to keep them on track and generally ensure that the reforms are carried out effectively.

In-service training can take numerous forms – general awareness training for all, detailed instruction for some. It can be provided at higher education institutions or within schools. It can be part of teachers' formal professional development or it can be pursued by individual teachers as a personal initiative.

What is important is that schools take responsibility for the professional development of their staff. This entails helping individual teachers to identify their training needs and creating a framework of opportunity within which those needs can be met. Particularly where integration is concerned, schools cannot afford to duck out of this responsibility. Unless all teachers acquire and maintain appropriate levels of competence, many pupils will not receive an education of high quality and integration will fail.

Next to teacher competence, the availability of appropriate support ranks high in the list of factors affecting teachers' ability to educate pupils with special needs in regular schools. The requisite support can be provided from within the school or by external staff. Ideally, both forms of support should be available: internal support can be closely matched to schools' specific requirements, whereas external agencies can provide a wider range of support than any one school can offer from its own resources.

Many schools find it helpful to designate a member of staff who has particular responsibility for special educational needs. This person will normally have received additional training. The way in which this teacher is deployed and carries out tasks will vary with the size of the school, the number of pupils with special needs on roll and the nature of their learning difficulties. The tasks are likely to include some or all of the following: advising other teachers on curriculum materials and teaching approaches; disseminating information on individual pupils' learning difficulties, and drawing attention to any significant changes in their situation; providing supplementary teaching for individual pupils; joining another teacher's class to provide support in the course of a lesson; promoting colleagues' professional development either directly themselves or by arranging in-service activities; liaising with external agencies; and carrying out the numerous administrative tasks that are necessary.

External support is necessary to give schools access to the range of expertise that teaching pupils with special needs requires. This must encompass assessment, advice, specialist teaching input and therapy. When children have complex learning difficulties multidisciplinary assessment that brings together the insights of different specialists is required to gain an understanding of their learning situation and assemble information to inform teaching. In most countries psychological services generally have a key input here, with other specialists contributing as appropriate. Learning support services are often established on an area basis to advise teachers on curriculum and organisational matters, monitor individual pupils' progress, provide specialist teaching as necessary and assist in staff development. For certain pupils speech therapy and physiotherapy are important elements of their educational programme, and arrangements need to be made to secure access to therapy and integrate it with the rest of pupils' work at school.

A further factor that facilitates integration relates to the curriculum. The segregation entailed in special schooling has often been magnified by the fact that special schools have had different curricula from regular schools. (In a few cases, notably where large numbers of pupils attend special schools, this differentiation does not occur. Thus, in the Netherlands the curriculum in schools for learning disabled pupils is more or less similar to the curriculum in regular schools.) This absence of a common curriculum framework institutionalises the separateness of the two sectors and makes integration more difficult to achieve.

Having a common curriculum which all pupils follow facilitates integration. It is not to be expected that all pupils will be doing the same work – that simply would not be realistic – but a common curriculum framework where the different educational programmes the pupils follow can be related to each other through common curricular principles is feasible. Such a framework makes it possible for pupils of different abilities to work alongside each other. It also provides a shared language to discuss the curriculum. This makes it easier for teachers to communicate with their colleagues about educational programmes for pupils with learning difficulties and to ensure that they participate in common programmes of work to the greatest extent possible.

Establishing a common curriculum in this way is not an easy task. There is always a tension between articulating the curriculum in usable detail and marginalising particular pupils because too specific demands are made on them. This is particularly the case for pupils with severe and complex learning difficulties. However, the existence of a common framework and the determination to translate it into practice are two of the most potent tools a teacher can have in trying to achieve real integration, where pupils with special needs participate in the work being done by class peers in a regular school.

In this chapter and in the previous one we have focused on the factors contributing to successful integration policies and practices. In the next chapter we address the question of the quality of our body of knowledge concerning integration. What have we learned from our experiences and to what extent can our learning be improved? This implies a broad approach to the concept of integration in which the concept itself will be scrutinised.

10

RETHINKING THE COURSE OF INTEGRATION: WHAT CAN WE LEARN FROM THE PAST?

Jan Rispens

INTRODUCTION

Integration is the key concept of a broad international movement that started in the sixties. Its aim was to bring about a fundamental reform of the system of provision for the mentally ill and the severely mentally retarded, and of special education for pupils with special needs. This movement has been successful to a certain extent. In many countries provision for the mentally ill has changed considerably, due to the implementation of the concept of community-based mental health care. Institutions for the mentally retarded have changed as a result of three decades of debate about the concepts of normalisation and deinstitutionalisation. The evidence presented in this book demonstrates that the same holds for the field of special education. As a result of the integration movement, both the theory and the practice of special education for children with special needs have changed considerably. This is the case not only in countries with a one-track educational policy; even in countries with a two-track or a multi-track system the idea that students with special needs should remain in regular schools has become an accepted part of educational policy. In all of the countries described, segregated special education is a matter for concern and debate.

Despite this success there is growing evidence that the potential of integration is difficult to realise. In the preceding chapters it emerged that, even in countries well known for their advanced forms of integration, there are problems of implementation in the integrated settings. In a recent article about the education of deaf children in Italy, the conclusion is reached that for some of these children integration may not be the best solution because of the lack of expertise in regular schools (Bennati, 1992). In the description of the Swedish educational system (Chapter 4) we concluded that in some cases separate special groups are formed under the responsibility of the special teacher. This is a violation of the idea of integration to a certain extent. In the description of the system in the USA (Chapter 5) we noted that proponents of the so-called Regular Education Initiative (REI) argue that regular education should take full responsibility for all students with special needs. However, this reformulation of the integration movement occasions much debate. In a critical analysis Kauffman (1989) argues that the REI goes too far. One of his arguments is that regular education is not equipped to cater for all children with special needs.

On the basis of the country descriptions we conclude that, although much progress has been made in the direction of integration, there are many problems still to be solved. Several questions are still unanswered, like: Does integration mean the same for children with different kinds of special needs? Does integration in the school make sense even if we know that no appropriate jobs are available for students with special needs? Therefore, integration remains a controversial issue, which in most countries still dominates the debate about the future of special education.

It is interesting to note that the situation is the same in the related fields of mental health care and provision for the mentally retarded. Several authors in these fields conclude that deinstitutionalisation has failed (Isaac and Armat, 1990; Johnson, 1990). Johnson states that, although the idea of integration is attractive, it becomes ever clearer that it is difficult to achieve in practice. 'Our mistake was in thinking that to initiate the process was to complete it' (Johnson, 1990, p. 255). In other words, integration has not yet achieved its potential.

For these reasons rethinking the course of integration seems necessary. This calls for a clarification of the concept of integration and better understanding of the practical difficulties with regard to the implementation of integration. It is our conviction that analysis of the experiences with integration in different countries may contribute to this process of clarification. In this chapter we reflect briefly on what can be learnt from the past in order to derive benefit for the future.

THE CONCEPT OF INTEGRATION

Reviews of the literature on integration often start with the claim that no generally accepted definition of integration is available (Kobi, 1983; Möckel, 1989). What do we have in mind when we speak about integration: integration in the classroom, in the school or, ultimately, integration of handicapped persons in society? In the preceding chapters we used the typology of Kobi (1983) to classify different levels of integration. However, there is no consensus about the requirements that have to be met in order to qualify an experiment as a proper experiment in integration. As a consequence, experiments in integration can start on different levels (e.g. physical, social or curricular integration), with different aims (integration of students with special needs into the classroom versus an attempt to change the attitudes of the non-handicapped in order to contribute to the integration of handicapped persons into society), based on different motives (dissatisfaction with the quality of the existing system of special education versus the idea that one has to contribute to educational reform), for different types of handicaps (mildly retarded pupils only versus all types of handicaps), in different contexts (an educational system that has accepted integration versus an isolated attempt in a traditional, segregated system). All possible variants are called 'integration'. One of the consequences of this lack of clarity is that it is often difficult to evaluate the results of experiments in terms of their contribution to a common understanding of the implications of integration.

DIVERSITY IN INTEGRATION PRACTICES

In Chapter 8 we concluded that countries differ considerably with respect to the practice of integration. Several factors contribute to this situation. Integration has to be implemented in educational systems that are different from each other. Each of these systems has its own history and is a reflection of the social and cultural identity of a country. For that reason attitudes towards integration

135

will differ and, as a consequence, different practices of integration are to be expected. Our comparisons of countries have demonstrated the importance of contextual factors.

Implementing integration has far-reaching consequences for a regular school. Analyses of integration experiments make it clear that this holds especially true for the teacher, who is confronted with new demands. Teacher preparation and support are of paramount importance. Due to practical limitations, such as lack of money or time, the relevance of teacher preparation and support has sometimes been underestimated. What we can learn from integration experiments is that there are clear limits to what can be expected from the classroom teacher. This results in a variety of integration practices within the same integration model.

A third factor that contributes to the diversity in integration is a lack of clarity about the goals of integration and the means to achieve them. The experiences with integration show that under the heading 'integration' too many, and in a number of cases even conflicting, interests have to be served.

The diversity of integration makes it difficult to define the parameters of successful integration. As a consequence, there is no educational practice that can serve as the standard or at least as a generally accepted example of integration. Neither is there a simple, straightforward answer to the question: What can we learn from experiences with integration? We have to accept a certain amount of uncertainty about what integration is.

MOTIVES AND AIMS

One of the main reasons for the uncertainties with respect to integration is that many arguments are brought forward in support of it. They represent a diversity of motives and aims for integration. Based on each of these arguments different criteria can be formulated to evaluate the outcomes of integration. This is one of the main factors that contribute to the existing lack of clarity about what integration can achieve. Three groups of motives can be distinguished: integration as an answer to the growing dissatisfaction with separate special schooling, integration as a part of educational reform and integration as an ideological movement.

Dissatisfaction with the existing system of special education

One of the arguments in defence of traditional, segregated special education is that it guarantees a better quality of schooling for students with special needs, e.g. because of the availability of better qualified personnel and more opportunity for individualised instruction. Dissatisfaction with segregated special education arises from the fact that there is ample evidence that those claims are not always warranted. Efficacy studies generally do not demonstrate better performance (socially or academically) by students in special education (Carlberg and Kavale, 1980; Gottlieb, 1981).

Identification, diagnosis and classification of students with special needs constitute another set of issues closely related to segregated special education that causes much controversy.

Although these arguments refer to serious problems, it is clear that they are not solved by integration as such. What we can learn from integration experiments is that, for instance, better education and proper classification are not necessary outcomes of integration. If one aims at improvement of the quality of instruction for students with special needs, it is clear that an integrated setting is not a 'conditio sine qua non'. The same is true for identification and classification. Even in integrated educational settings identification of pupils who need extra attention will continue to be necessary.

Educational reform

The process of integration has been complicated, to a certain extent, by the fact that in many countries it has coincided with an extensive educational reform. For that reason attempts to integrate pupils with special needs are best seen as part of a broad educational innovation in which a 'modern' school system is implemented. In some of these cases integration was not primarily an attempt to improve the quality of education for children with special needs; it was rather a consequence of a school reform which sought to offer instruction geared to the needs of all students. Integration then provides one of the criteria for evaluating the quality of school reform. The case of the Regular Education Initiative in the USA demonstrates that the trend towards integration may be part of a change in educational policy (Hallahan *et al.*, 1988).

There is no reason to believe that integration that starts primarily as part of a reform of the educational system cannot be successful. However, there are several risks here. The most important is a lack of reflection about the consequences of the diversity within the group of children with special needs. Integration in this case is a top down process. Since it does not have its starting point in special education or expertise in the schooling of children with special needs, it is not unlikely that in this case integration implicitly means the integration of mildly handicapped pupils and pupils with learning disabilities. But what about the deaf, the blind and the severely physically disabled? Integration may not be the appropriate answer here. In other words, integration as an aspect of a broad educational reform is at risk of being accused of neglecting the specific interests of some categories of children with special needs. What we can learn here is that for some categories of children with special needs integration has to proceed with extreme caution.

Ideological motives

The philosophy underlying the initial attempts to integrate children with special needs into regular education stemmed from critical movements in the social sciences during the sixties. It is easy to sense this critical flavour in several arguments that still play a role in the integration debate. The idea that special education contributes to (later) stigmatisation is an example. Another illustration is found in the idea that handicaps are social constructs (Gelzheiser, 1987) or in the conviction that the organisation (i.e. the segregation) of special education is the cause of overrepresentation of children from ethnic and socio-economic minority groups (Bickel, 1982). Integration is supposed to be the answer to these problems.

However, this is a simplistic view of integration and one that ignores social realities. There is, for instance, some evidence that also in integrated settings stigmatisation of children with special needs occurs (Gottlieb, 1981). On the other hand, it can be argued that placement in regular settings is a minimum condition that must be met if the interaction between children with special needs and their peers is to be improved. It is a necessary but not a sufficient condition.

If integration is rooted in these ideological arguments, non-handicapped students are involved just as much as those who are handicapped. To this extent integration can be considered a success, at least in part, even if students with special needs do not benefit from it academically.

One of the consequences of the fact that ideology plays an important role in the integration movement is an increased risk of controversies and conflicts that are difficult to resolve (Gelzheiser, 1987). Facts are not decisive. In the event of disappointing results from integration experiments it can be argued that, even if none of the practical objectives has been achieved, there is no reason to discard the goals of integration and participation since these represent moral commitments. Several writers have a view of integration as emerging from a value system that should not (and cannot) be subjected to empirical testing, or argue that it is not the task of research to demonstrate that integration does not work (Greenspan and Cerreto, 1989).

In an analysis of controversies with respect to the concepts of normalisation and deinstitutionalisation (cognate concepts from the field of care for the mentally retarded), Landesman and Butterfield (1987) conclude: 'Controversy about normalisation and deinstitutionalisation will continue and will not be abated by any amount of scientific inquiry. The controversy is based on differences in faith, experience, and values, and the relative validity of the different positions is untestable' (p. 814).

CONCLUSION

From our country descriptions it has become clear that although integration plays an important role in special education, not all its objectives have been achieved. Even in countries that strive towards an integrated educational system there is a good deal of uncertainty as to whether integration is appropriate for all categories of children with special needs. Furthermore, it is clear that even in these countries there are many practical problems in the daily practice of integration.

One of the main lessons that can be learnt is that there is no standardised format for integration. Every aspect of integration – definition, motives, aims and level – shows a large diversity in practice. This diversity makes it difficult to draw overall conclusions and build up a comprehensive understanding of integration. Rethinking the course and the content of integration seems necessary. Experiences from the past can contribute to this reflection if the objectives and motives behind integration are set out more clearly.

11

EPILOGUE

The country descriptions in this book show a large diversity of organisational models, expertise and experiences in the attempt to reduce segregation of students with special needs in education. Our goal in writing this book was to describe this diversity and to evaluate the outcomes in order to extend our knowledge base on integration and profit from each other's experiences.

In the last three chapters we chose different perspectives to describe and evaluate the outcomes of this study. In the section 'Quantitative aspects of integration' (Chapter 8), an overview is given of our findings concerning countries' integration policies: policy tracks, number of students labelled and the 'one per cent group' that is difficult to integrate in curricular terms.

In the section 'Qualitative aspects of integration' (Chapter 8), a number of suggestions are made to facilitate the process of integration. The suggestions are all focused on organisational measures: restating the responsibilities of teachers, getting rid of labelling procedures and making selective use of special classes in regular schools.

In Chapter 9, the focus is on the teacher. In the end it is the teacher who 'transforms' all laws, regulations, resources, support and curriculum frameworks into an instructional offering to all students in the classroom; the teacher is the key mediating factor. In Chapter 9, Hegarty spells out a number of factors that bear on the teacher's willingness and ability to provide appropriate education for pupils with special needs. The factors discussed are: the nature of society, conceptions of disability, school financing mechanisms, teacher competences, the support available to teachers and the curriculum.

141

Chapter 10 returns to the concept of integration. Rispens argues that definitions, motives and levels of integration vary widely. The lack of clear operational definitions of integration hampers evaluation research and thus the building of a knowledge base on integration. This lack is clearly reflected in most of the country descriptions included in this book. With the exception of the USA, one can state that evaluation of integration is scarce. This scarcity of data makes it difficult to decide on adjustments to the ongoing integration process. Decisions by policy makers, teacher trainers, support personnel and teachers have to be based on rather limited evidence.

Yet, despite the limited evaluation data and the problems involved in comparisons between countries, an attempt has been made to learn from the information gathered in this investigation. It is our belief that, notwithstanding the problems and the criticisms made in this book, impressive progress has been made in several countries in the process of integrating students with special needs into ordinary education. In the coming decade it is to be hoped that this progress will be maintained and that many more regular schools will provide an education of high quality for pupils with special needs.

BIBLIOGRAPHY

Abbring, I. M., Meijer, C. J. W., and Rispens, J. (1989a) *Landenstudies. Het Onderwijs aan Leerlingen met Problemen in Internationaal Perspectief*, Eerste rapport van het CASE-project, Groningen: RION.
—— (1989b) *Landenstudies. Integratie in de Praktijk*, Tweede rapport van het CASE-project, Groningen: RION.
Abeson, A. and Zettel, J. (1981) 'The end of a quiet revolution: the United States for All Handicapped Children Act, 1975', in W. Swann (ed.) *The Practice of Special Education* (359–77), Oxford: Basil Blackwell and the Open University Press.
Affleck, J. Q., Madge, S., Adams, A., and Lowenbraun, S. (1988) 'Integrated classroom versus resource model: academic viability and effectiveness', *Exceptional Children* 54, 4: 339–48.
Algozzine, B., Morsink, C. V., and Algozzine, K. M. (1988) 'What's happening in self-contained special education classrooms?', *Exceptional Children* 55, 3: 259–65.
Antal, A. B., Dierkes, M., and Weiler, H. N. (1987) 'Cross-national policy research: traditions, achievements and challenges', in M. Dierkes, H. N. Weiler, and A. B. Antal (eds) *Comparative Policy Research* (13–25), Aldershot: Gower.
ARBO (1984) *Het Moet Ons een Zorg Zijn. Advies over Zorgverbreding in het Basisonderwijs*, Zeist: ARBO, Onderwijscentrum Zeist.
Baker, J. and Zigmond, N. (1989) *Snapshots of an Elementary School: are Regular Education Classes Equipped to Accommodate LD Students?*, project report, Pittsburgh: University of Pittsburgh.
—— (1990) 'Are regular education classes equipped to accommodate students with learning disabilities?', *Exceptional Children* 56, 6: 515–26.
Bateman, B. D. and Herr, C. M. (1981) 'Law and special education', in D. P. Hallahan and J. M. Kauffman (eds) *The Handbook of Special Education* (330–60), Englewood Cliffs: Prentice Hall.
Bennati, M. (1992) 'Dovenonderwijs in Italië', *Speciaal Onderwijs* 65, 4: 124–30.
Bianchi, M. G. (1984) 'Lehrerbildung für den Unterricht behinderter Kinder in Italien', in B. Döbrich, C. Kodron, J. Lynch, and W. Mitter (eds)

Lehrerbildung für den Unterricht behinderter Kinder in ausgewählten Ländern (1–64), Cologne: Böhlau Verlag.

Bickel, W. (1982) 'Classifying mentally retarded students: a review of placement practices in special education', in K. A. Heller, W. H. Holtzman, and S. Messick (eds) *Placing Children in Special Education. A Strategy for Equity* (182–231), Washington DC: National Academy Press.

Blake, M. E. (1984) 'Reading in Denmark: a relaxed atmosphere is the key', *The Reading Teacher* 38, 1: 42–47.

Boer, K. den (1990) 'Country briefing. Special education in the Netherlands', *European Journal of Special Needs Education* 5, 2: 136–49.

Bowman, I., Wedell, K., and Wedell, N. (1985) *Helping Handicapped Pupils in Ordinary Schools: Strategies for Teacher Training*, Paris: UNESCO.

Brown, B. W. and Saks, D. H. (1987) 'The micro-economics of the allocation of teachers' time and student learning', *Economics of Education Review* 6, 4: 319–32.

Bruun, I. and Koefoed, E. (1982) *Handicapped Persons in Denmark*, Copenhagen: Statens Laereruddannelse.

Bürli, A. (1985) *Zur Behindertenpädagogik in Italien, England und Dänemark*, Luzern: Verlag der Schweizerischen Zentralstelle für Heilpädagogik.

Carlberg, C. G. and Kavale, K. (1980) 'The efficacy of special versus regular class placement for exceptional children: a meta-analysis', *Journal of Special Education* 14, 3: 295–309.

Carnine, D. W. and Kameenui, E. J. (1990) 'The general education initiative and children with special needs: a false dilemma in the face of true problems', *Journal of Learning Disabilities* 23, 3: 141–48.

Claessens, W. J. (1990) 'Ambulante begeleiding en zorgverbreding' in M. K. van der Heijden and J. Rispens (eds) *Zorgverbreding en Afgrenzing* (80–86), Amsterdam: Swets and Zeitlinger.

Claessens, W. J., Vries, E. M. de, Eijk, G. E. M. van, and Bertens, J. (1989) *Ambulante Begeleiding. Een Beschrijvend Onderzoek naar de Vormgeving en Inhoud van Ambulante Begeleiding*, De Lier: Academisch Boeken Centrum.

Coates, R. D. (1989) 'The regular education initiative and opinions of regular classroom teachers', *Journal of Learning Disabilities* 22, 9: 532–36.

Danish Ministry of Education (1983) *Education (Local Administration) Act*, Copenhagen: Danish Ministry of Education.

—— (1988a) *Handicapped Students in the Danish Educational System*, Copenhagen: Danish Ministry of Education.

—— (1988b) *Education Statistics*, Copenhagen: Danish Ministry of Education.

—— (1991a) *The Development of the Danish Public School Towards a School for All*, Copenhagen: Danish Ministry of Education.

—— (1991b) *Act on the Folkeskole*, Copenhagen: Danish Ministry of Education.

—— (1991c) *Administration of the Folkeskole*, Copenhagen: Danish Ministry of Education.

—— (1991d) *Handicapped Students in the Danish Educational System*, Copenhagen: Danish Ministry of Education.

Danish Ministry of Education (1992) *Contribution from Denmark to 'The Synthesis Report on Integration'*, Copenhagen: Danish Ministry of Education.

Deen, N. (1983) 'Onderwijs in Noord-Amerika', *Losbladig Onderwijskundig Lexicon* ST 5100–3–5100–21, Alphen a/d Rijn: Samsom.

Department of Education (1990) *Twelfth Annual Report to Congress on the Implementation of The Education of the Handicapped Act*, Washington: US Department of Education.

Department of Education and Science (DES) (1978) *Special Educational Needs (Warnock Report)*, London: HMSO.

Döbrich, P., Kodron, C., Lynch, J., and Mitter, W. (1984) *Lehrerbildung für den Unterricht behinderter Kinder in ausgewählten Ländern*, Cologne: Böhlau Verlag.

Eklindh, K. (1985) *Special Education in Sweden*, Stockholm: Swedish National Board of Education.

Emanuelsson, I. (1985) *Integration of Handicapped Pupils in Sweden: Concepts, Research Experiences, Present Practices*, Stockholm: Swedish National Board of Education.

Epps, S. and Tindal, G. (1987) 'The effectiveness of differential programming in serving students with mild handicaps', in M. C. Wang, M. C. Reynolds, and H. J. Walberg (eds) *Handbook of Special Education, Vol. 1* (213–48), Oxford: Pergamon Press.

Eurydice (1983) *L'anno nell'Educazione e nella Formazione, 10. Collana di Testi e Documenti*, Brussel: Eurydice.

—— (1986) *The Education Structures in the Member States of the European Communities*, Brussels: Eurydice European Unit.

Ferro, N. (1992) Written communication to the Institute for Educational Research, RION.

Fuchs, D. and Fuchs, L. S. (1988) 'Evaluation of the adaptive learning environments model', *Exceptional Children* 55, 2: 115–27.

Galliani, L. (1982) 'Situation und Probleme der Sonderpädagogik in Italien', *Zeitschrift für Heilpädagogik* 33, 4: 193–203.

Gelzheiser, L. M. (1987) 'Reducing the number of students identified as learning disabled: a question of practice, philosophy, or policy?', *Exceptional Children* 54, 2: 145–50.

Gerber, M. M. and Semmel, M. I. (1984) 'Teacher as imperfect test: reconceptualizing the referral process', *Educational Psychologist* 19, 3: 137–48.

—— (1985) 'The microeconomics of referral and reintegration: a paradigm for evaluation of special education', *Studies in Educational Evaluation* 11, 1: 13–29.

Goacher, B., Evans, J., Welton, J., and Wedell, K. (1988) *Policy and Provision for Special Educational Needs: Implementing the 1991 Education Act*, London: Cassell.

Gottlieb, J. (1981) 'Mainstreaming: fulfilling the promise?', *American Journal of Mental Deficiency* 86, 2: 115–26.

Gran, B. (1986) 'The comprehensive schools in Sweden from primary to secondary education', in W. Wielemans (ed.) *Vernieuwingen in het Secundair Onderwijs*, Leuven: Acco.

Greenspan, S. and Cerreto, M. (1989) 'Normalization, deinstitutionalization, and the limits of research', *American Psychologist* 44, 2: 448–49.

Grundin, H. U. (1979) 'Remedial education: a Swedish viewpoint', *Remedial Education* 14, 2: 74–78.

Guidi, E. (1986) *Risposta al Quesito NL 8500600*, Firenze: Biblioteca di Documentazione Pedagogica, Unità Italiana di Eurydice.

Hallahan, D. P., Keller, C. E., McKinney, J. D., Lloyd, J. W., and Bryan, T. (1988) 'Examining the research base of the Regular Education Initiative. Efficacy studies and the adaptive learning environments model', *Journal of Special Education* 21, 1: 29–36.

Hansen, J. (undated) *Educational Provision in Denmark*, Copenhagen: Ministry of Education.

—— (1992) 'The development of the Danish Folkeskole towards a school for all', *European Journal of Special Needs Education* 7, 1: 38–46.

Hayes, H. and Le Metais, J. (1991) *The Management of Compulsory Education in England and Wales: an Outline of Responsibilities*, Slough: NFER.

Hegarty, S. (1993) *Meeting Special Needs in Ordinary Schools*, London: Cassell.

Hegarty, S., Pocklington, K., and Lucas, D. (1981) *Educating Pupils with Special Needs in the Ordinary School*, Windsor: NFER-Nelson.

Isaac, R. J. and Armat, V. C. (1990) *Madness in the Streets*, New York: Free Press.

Jencks, C. S. (1972) *Inequality: A Reassessment of the Effect of Family and Schooling in America*, New York: Basic Books.

Jenkins, J. R., Pious, C. G., and Jewell, M. (1990) 'Special education and the Regular Education Initiative: basic assumptions', *Exceptional Children* 56, 6: 479–91.

Jenkins, J. R. and Pious, C. G. (1991) 'Full inclusion and the REI: a reply to Thousand and Villa', *Exceptional Children* 57, 6: 562–64.

Johnson, A. B. (1990) *Out of the Bedlam*, New York: Basic Books.

Jørgensen, I. S. (1979) *Special Education in Denmark*, Copenhagen: Ministry of Education.

—— (1980) *Het Buitengewoon Onderwijs in de Europese Gemeenschap*, Luxemburg: Bureau voor officiële publikaties der Europese Gemeenschappen.

Jowett, S., Hegarty, S., and Moses, D. (1988) *Joining Forces: A Study of Links between Special and Ordinary Schools*, Windsor: NFER-Nelson.

Juul, K. D. (1987) 'Vereinigte Staaten von Amerika (USA)', in K. Klauer and W. Mitter (eds) *Vergleichende Sonderpädagogik, Handbuch Sonderpädagogik, Band II* (565–86), Berlin: Carl Marhold Verlagsbuchhandlung.

Kauffman, J. M. (1989) 'The Regular Education Initiative as Reagan–Bush education policy. A trickle-down theory of education of the hard-to-teach', *Journal of Special Education* 23, 3: 256–79.

Kauffman, J. M., Gerber, M. M., and Semmel, M. I. (1988) 'Arguable assumptions underlying the Regular Education Initiative', *Journal of Learning Disabilities* 21, 1: 6–11.

Keogh, B. K. (1988) 'Improving services for problem learners: rethinking and restructuring', *Journal of Learning Disabilities* 21, 1: 19–22.

Kobi, E. E. (1983) 'Praktizierte Integration: eine Zwischenbilanz', *Vierteljahresschrift für Heilpädagogik und ihre Nachbargebiete* 52, 2: 196–216.

Kool, E. and Wolfgram, H. P. (1987) *Evaluatie Zorgverbredingsprojecten*, Den Haag: SVO.

Kropveld, P. (1983) 'Kan het zonder? Een moment van de Italiaanse zorgbreedte', *Speciaal* 4: 24–25.

Landesman, S. J. and Butterfield, E. C. (1987) 'Normalization and deinstitutionalization of mentally retarded individuals', *American Psychologist* 42, 8: 809–16.

Leinhardt, G., Bickel, W., and Pallay, A. (1982) 'Unlabeled but still entitled: toward more effective remediation', *Teachers College Records* 84, 2: 391–422.

Lewis, A. (1991) *Primary Special Needs and the National Curriculum*, London: Routledge.

Lunetta, F. (1987) 'Italien', in K. J. Klauer and W. Mitter (eds) *Vergleichende Sonderpädagogik, Handbuch Sonderpädagogik, Band II* (170–85), Berlin: Carl Marhold Verlagsbuchhandlung.

Madge, S., Affleck, J., and Lowenbraun, S. (1990) 'Social effects of integrated classroom and resource room regular class placements on elementary students with learning difficulties', *Journal of Learning Disabilities* 23, 7: 439–45.

Magne, O. (1987) 'Skandinavien', in K. J. Klauer and W. Mitter (eds) *Vergleichende Sonderpädagogik, Handbuch Sonderpädagogik, Band II* (316–36), Berlin: Carl Marhold Verlagsbuchhandlung.

Meijer, C. J. W. (1988) *Verwijzing gewogen*, dissertatie RU Leiden, Groningen: RION.

Meijer, C. J. W., Pijl, S. J., and Kramer, L. J. L. M. (1989) 'Rekenen met groei. Ontwikkelingen in de deelname aan het (voortgezet) speciaal onderwijs (1972–1987)', *Tijdschrift voor Orthopedagogiek* 28, 2: 71–82.

Ministerie van Onderwijs en Wetenschappen (1989) *Rijkdom van het Onvoltooide. Uitdagingen voor het Nederlandse Onderwijs*, Den Haag: SDU.

—— (1990) *Weer samen naar school*, Den Haag: SDU.

Ministero della Pubblica Istruzione (1985) *Rilevazione Statistica nella Scuola Materna, Elementare e Media dell' Obbligio. Ani scolastici 1979/80 – 1984/85*, Rome: Ministero della Pubblica Instruzione, Ufficio studi e programmazione.

—— (1990) 'Education Statistics', in L. de Anna, *Une Vie Active pour les Adolescents Porteurs de Handicap. L'intégration à l'École*, rapport sur la 1e phase du project OCDE.

Mittler, P. (1988) 'Special education in Britain', paper presented for the Japanese Teachers' Association, Tokyo, Manchester: University of Manchester.

Möckel, A. (1989) 'Integration, Unterrichtskompetenz und Schulaufsicht', *Zeitschrift für Heilpädagogik* 40, 11: 745–55.

Newell, P. (1983) *ACE Special Education Handbook: The New Laws on Children with Special Needs*, London: Advisory Centre for Education.

Niessen, M. and Peschar, J. (eds) (1982) *International Comparative Research. Problems of Theory, Methodology and Organisation in Eastern and Western Europe*, Oxford: Pergamon Press.

OECD (1979) *Educational Financing and Policy Goals for Primary Schools, Vol. III*, Paris: OECD.

—— (1980) *Educational Policy and Planning: Goals for Educational Policy in Sweden*, Paris: OECD.

—— (1981a) *Reviews of National Policies for Education: Educational Reforms in Sweden*, Paris: OECD.

—— (1981b) *United States. Federal Policies for Education for the Disadvantaged*, Paris: OECD.

—— (1985) *Educational Reforms in Italy*, Paris: OECD.

Øyen, E. (1990) 'The imperfection of comparisons', in E. Øyen (ed.) *Comparative Methodology* (1–18), London: Sage.

Pijl, S. J. and Blaauboer, S. A. A. (1990) *Werken met Handelingsplannen*, Groningen: RION.

Pijl, S. J., Graaf, S. de, and Emanuelsson, I. (1988) 'The function of individualized education programmes in special education: a discussion of premises', *European Journal of Special Needs Education* 3, 2: 63–73.

Pijl, S. J. and Meijer, C. J. W. (1991) 'Does integration count for much? An analysis of the practices of integration in eight countries', *European Journal of Special Needs Education* 6, 2: 100–12.

—— (1992) 'The integration concept: reflections on Daunt', *European Journal of Special Needs Education* 7, 1: 36–37.

Pugach, M. C. (1985) 'The limitations of federal special education policy: the role of classroom teachers in determining who is handicapped', *Journal of Special Education* 19, 1: 123–37.

Reynolds, M. C. (1990) 'Noncategorical Special Education', in M. C. Wang, M. C. Reynolds, and H. J. Walberg (eds) *Special Education: Research and Practice* (57–80), Oxford: Pergamon Press.

Reynolds, M. C., Wang, M. C., and Walberg, H. J. (1987) 'The necessary restructuring of special and regular education', *Exceptional Children* 53, 5: 391–98.

Roser, L. O. (1981) 'Keine Aussonderung Behinderten: gemeinsam leben und lernen', *Behindertenpädagogik* 20, 1: 18–23.

Semmel, M. I., Abernathy, T. V., Butera, G., and Lesar S. (1991) 'Teacher perceptions of the Regular Education Initiative', *Exceptional Children* 58, 1: 9–24.

Shinn, M., Tindal, G. A., and Spira, D. A. (1987) 'Special education referrals as an index of teacher tolerance: are teachers imperfect tests?', *Exceptional Children* 54, 1: 32–40.

Singer, J. D. and Butler, J. A. (1987) 'The Education for All Handicapped Children Act: schools as agents of social reform', *Harvard Educational Review* 57, 2: 125–52.

Söder, M. (1984) *Integration in School and Transition from School to Work for*

Handicapped Adolescents, Swedish country report to the OECD/CERI project on education of the handicapped adolescent, Stockholm.

Statistiska Centralbyrån (1986) *Utbildningsstatistisk årsbok*, Stockholm: Statistiska Centralbyrån.

Stokking, K. M. (1990) 'Zorgverbreding en differentiatie op basisscholen en nascholing lezen', in M. K. van der Heijden and J. Rispens (eds) *Zorgverbreding en Afgrenzing* (28–36), Amsterdam: Swets and Zeitlinger.

Swedish National Board of Education (1982) *Helping Pupils in Difficulty*, Stockholm: Swedish National Board of Education.

—— (1985) *Special School Curriculum*, Stockholm: Swedish National Board of Education.

Thannhäuser, A. (1983) 'Integration behinderter Kinder in Italien – Eine Reisebericht', *Behindertenpädagogik* 22, 4: 306–59.

Vinjé, M. P. (1990) 'De invloed van het zorgverbredingsbeleid op de leerprestaties van kinderen', in M. K. van der Heijden and J. Rispens (eds) *Zorgverbreding en Afgrenzing* (17–25), Amsterdam: Swets and Zeitlinger.

Voelker Morsink, C., Chase Thomas, C. C., and Smith-Davis, J. (1987) 'Noncategorical special education programs: process and outcomes', in M. C. Wang, M. C. Reynolds, and H. J. Walberg (eds) *Handbook of Special Education: Research and Practice, Vol. 1*, New York: Pergamon Press.

Wang, M. C. and Birch, J. W. (1984a) 'Comparison of a full-time mainstreaming program and a resource room approach', *Exceptional Children* 51, 1: 33–40.

—— (1984b) 'Effective special education in regular classes', *Exceptional Children* 50, 5: 391–98.

Wang, M. C., Gennari, P., and Waxman, H. C. (1985) 'The adaptive learning environments model: design, implementation and effects', in M. C. Wang and H. J. Walberg (eds) *Adapting Instruction to Individual Differences* (191–235), Berkeley: McCutchan.

Wang, M. C., Peverly, S., and Randolph, R. (1984) 'An investigation of the implementation and effects of a full-time mainstreaming program', *Remedial and Special Education* 5, 6: 21–32.

Weatherley, R. and Lipsky, M. (1981) 'Street-level bureaucrats and institutional innovation: implementing special educational reform', in W. Swann (ed.) *The Practice of Special Education* (378–97), Oxford: Basil Blackwell and the Open University Press.

Wedell, K. (1990) 'The 1988 Act and current principles', in H. Daniels and J. Ware (eds) *Special Educational Needs and the National Curriculum: the Impact of the Education Reform Act* (1–10), London: Kogan Page.

Wielemans, F. J. W. (1987) 'De ontwikkeling van het onderwijs in Italië', *Losbladig Onderwijskundig Lexicon* ST 3210–1–ST3210–10, Alphen a/d Rijn: Samsom.

Will, M. (1986) *Educating Students with Learning Problems: a Shared Responsibility*, Washington DC: US Department of Education.

Wolfendale, S. (1982) 'The education of handicapped children in the U. S. A. An outline of Public law 94–142 and its relevance to policy and practice in Britain', *Remedial Education* 17, 1: 32–34.

Wood, S. W. and MacDonald, M. (1988) *Project MERGE*. Project report, Olympia: Olympia School District.

Ysseldyke, J. E. (1987) 'Classification of handicapped students', in M. C. Wang, M. C. Reynolds, and H. J. Walberg (eds) *Handbook of Special Education: Research and Practice Vol. 1* (253–71), New York: Pergamon Press.

Ysseldyke, J. E. and Algozzine, B. (1982) *Critical Issues in Special and Remedial Education*, Boston: Houghton Mifflin.

Zigmond, N. and Baker, J. (1990) 'Mainstream experiences for learning disabled students (project MELD): preliminary report', *Exceptional Children 57*, 2: 176–85.

NAME INDEX

SUBJECT INDEX